A gift from:
Friends of the
Pinole Library

EXPLORERS AND EXPLORATION

4

ERATOSTHENES OF CYRENE – GUDRID

Marshall Cavendish
New York • London • Singapore

Marshall Cavendish
99 White Plains Road
Tarrytown, New York 10591-9001

www.marshallcavendish.com

Consultants: Ralph Ehrenberg, former chief, Geography and Map Division, Library of Congress, Washington, DC; Conrad Heidenreich, former historical geography professor, York University, Toronto; Shane Winser, information officer, Royal Geographical Society, London

Contributing authors: Dale Anderson, Kay Barnham, Peter Chrisp, Richard Dargie, Paul Dowswell, Elizabeth Gogerly, Conrad Heidenreich, Steven Maddocks, John Malam, Stewart Ross, Shane Winser

MARSHALL CAVENDISH
Editor: Thomas McCarthy
Editorial Director: Paul Bernabeo
Production Manager: Michael Esposito

WHITE-THOMSON PUBLISHING
Editors: Alex Woolf and Steven Maddocks
Design: Derek Lee and Ross George
Cartographer: Peter Bull Design
Picture Research: Glass Onion Pictures
Indexer: Fiona Barr

ISBN 0-7614-7535-4 (set)
ISBN 0-7614-7539-7 (vol. 4)

Printed in China

08 07 06 05 04 5 4 3 2 1

color key	time period
▬	to 500
▬	500–1400
▬	1400–1850
▬	1850–1945
▬	1945–2000
▬	general articles

Library of Congress Cataloging-in-Publication Data
Explorers and exploration.
p. cm.
Includes bibliographical references (p.) and index.
ISBN 0-7614-7535-4 (set : alk. paper) -- ISBN 0-7614-7536-2 (v. 1) -- ISBN 0-7614-7537-0 (v. 2) -- ISBN 0-7614-7538-9 (v. 3) -- ISBN 0-7614-7539-7 (v. 4) -- ISBN 0-7614-7540-0 (v. 5) -- ISBN 0-7614-7541-9 (v. 6) -- ISBN 0-7614-7542-7 (v. 7) -- ISBN 0-7614-7543-5 (v. 8) -- ISBN 0-7614-7544-3 (v. 9) -- ISBN 0-7614-7545-1 (v. 10) -- ISBN 0-7614-7546-X (v. 11)
1. Explorers--Encyclopedias. 2. Discoveries in geography--Encyclopedias. I. Marshall Cavendish Corporation. II. Title.
G80.E95 2005
910'.92'2--dc22
2004048292

ILLUSTRATION CREDITS

AKG London: 245, 248 (Statens Historiska Museum, Stockholm), 272, 284 (Bodleian Library, Oxford, UK), 289 (Jean-Louis Nou), 297, 298 (Rheinisches Landesmuseum, Trier, Germany), 304 (Stadelsches Kunstinstitut, Frankfurt am Main), 317 (Jürgen Sorges).

Bridgeman Art Library: 244, 247 (British Library, London), 251 (Lincolnshire County Council, Usher Gallery, Lincoln, UK), 252 (Ken Welsh), 257, 260, 261 (Library of Congress, Washington, DC), 262 (INDEX), 263, 264 (Royal Naval College, Greenwich, London), 266 (Michael Graham-Stewart), 268 (Mitchell Library, State Library of New South Wales), 270 (Stapleton Collection, UK), 274, 275, 291, 293, 295, 299 (British Museum, London), 300 (University Library, Istanbul), 301 (Index / Bibliothèque Nationale, Paris), 302 (Index), 303 (Lauros / Giraudon / Bibliothèque Nationale, Paris), 313, 314 (National Library of Australia, Canberra), 318 (Arni Magnusson Institute, Reykjavik, Iceland).

Genesis Space Photo Library: 306, 307, 308 (NASA).

Peter Newark's American Pictures: 271, 273, 275, 276, 279, 280, 281, 282, 312.

Peter Newark's Historical Pictures: 265, 286, 288, 290.

Royal Geographical Society: 253, 254, 315.

Science and Society Picture Library: 310 (NASA).

Science Photo Library: 311 (Ken M. Johns).

Topham Picturepoint: 267 (Science Museum, London).

Peter van der Krogt: 316.

Werner Forman Archive: 250, 256 (N. J. Saunders), 298.

Cover: German compass, sixteenth-century (AKG London / Kunstgewerbemuseum, Berlin).

Contents

Eratosthenes of Cyrene

THE GREEK MATHEMATICIAN AND GEOGRAPHER Eratosthenes, born between 285 and 276 BCE in Cyrene (present-day Shahhat, Libya), was a leading scholar of his day who became head of the library at Alexandria, Egypt. Among his many achievements were the calculation of the circumference of the earth and detailed descriptions of its geography. In old age Eratosthenes went blind, and some believe that he starved himself to death around 194 BCE.

Below **This seventeenth-century-CE engraving of Eratosthenes is based on pure guesswork: it is not known what he looked like.**

An Educated Man

Known as a center of literature and learning, Cyrene was a wealthy Greek colonial city in North Africa where several of the most prominent scholars of the day were educated. Few details survive of the early life of Eratosthenes. As a young man he was educated by the city's foremost teachers. Lysanias of Cyrene taught him philology, the study of the origin, meaning, and use of words (in his case in the Greek language). Callimachus of Cyrene, the author of more than eight hundred books, taught him Greek literature and poetry. At some point Eratosthenes left Cyrene and continued his education in Athens, where he studied philosophy.

Eratosthenes the Librarian

After studying in Athens for several years, Eratosthenes was offered the job of director of the library at Alexandria on the northern coast of Egypt, one of the largest and grandest cities in the entire Mediterranean region. As well as taking up the position of head of the city's library (which housed an estimated 500,000 handwritten scrolls), Eratosthenes was also appointed personal tutor to the Greek-speaking king of Egypt, Ptolemy III (reigned 246–221 BCE), and his young son, Philopater. A great many scholars lived in Alexandria, and Eratosthenes must have felt at home among them. He was given the nicknames Pentathlos ("all-rounder") and Beta ("B-class," or "second best")—references to his broad knowledge but also to the fact that he was not considered the cleverest person in town.

Left **From the third century BCE, the library at Alexandria was the scientific and cultural center of the world. Ptolemy III (reigned 246–221 BCE) was determined that the library should house a copy of every text in existence. In time the library collected about 700,000 manuscripts, stored as papyrus rolls. All were lost in the late fourth century CE when the library burned to the ground.**

Calculating the Earth's Circumference

Eratosthenes made a major contribution to understanding of the physical world. When he observed that the sun shone straight down a deep-water well at Syene (present-day Aswan) in southern Egypt at noon on the same day each year, he used this fact to calculate the earth's polar circumference (the distance around the earth along a line that passes through the North and South Poles).

c. 285–276 BCE
Eratosthenes is born at Cyrene, North Africa.

c. 234 BCE
Becomes chief librarian at Alexandria, Egypt.

c. 245 BCE
Measures the polar circumference of the earth.

c. 245–c. 200 BCE
Produces a world map; writes books on mathematics, history, philosophy, and poetry, all of which are now lost.

c. 194 BCE
Dies in Alexandria.

How Eratosthenes Measured the Earth

Eratosthenes found out that at noon on the summer solstice (around June 21) the sun shone directly down on Syene, Egypt, casting no shadows on the ground. At the same time the sun's rays caused a small shadow to be cast by an obelisk at Alexandria. Eratosthenes calculated the shadow's angle to be 7.2 degrees. As a circle the earth's circumference consists of 360 degrees. Thus, the angle of the obelisk's shadow was one-fiftieth of the circumference of the earth. Next he calculated the distance from Syene to Alexandria as 5,000 stades—one stade being equal to 517 feet (157.58 m)—and multiplied this number by 50. The resulting figure of 250,000 stades was the north-south, or polar, circumference of the planet, which he later adjusted to 252,000 stades, or 24,675 miles (39,710 km).

The philosopher Pythagoras, who lived during the sixth century BCE, had been the first to make the claim that the world was a sphere. Although this belief was becoming widely accepted, it was not until the work of Eratosthenes that the claim could be proved and some measure of the earth's size could be gained.

In *On the Measurement of the Earth,* Eratosthenes described how he had measured the earth's circumference. Like all the works of Eratosthenes, the original text is now lost, but because parts of the text survive in citations by other ancient authors, it is possible to work out how Eratosthenes produced his calculation. The figure he arrived at, 24,675 miles (39,710 km), compares remarkably well with the modern measurement for the earth's polar circumference of 24,860 miles (40,000 km). For the first time in history, with the true size of the earth calculated, the Greeks were able to visualize what proportion of the entire world was known to them.

Eratosthenes the Geographer

In his *Geographica* Eratosthenes described the world known to him and to the people of his time. He compiled the *Geographica* after consulting a number of texts held in the library at Alexandria. His sources included the reports of Alexander the Great's surveyors in Asia and the narratives of such travelers as Megasthenes (c. 350–290 BCE), who described parts of India; Nearchus, who sailed around India in the fourth century BCE; and Pytheas of Massalia (c. 380–310 BCE), who sailed northward on a voyage that reached Britain and possibly even Iceland.

In *Geographica* Eratosthenes wrote about the world in terms of its land, its seas, and its people. He included a map of the world that stretched from western France to the Ganges River in India and from the island of Thule (Iceland) in the north to the supposed sources of the Nile River in Africa. The world was envisaged as an elongated rectangle surrounded on all sides by ocean.

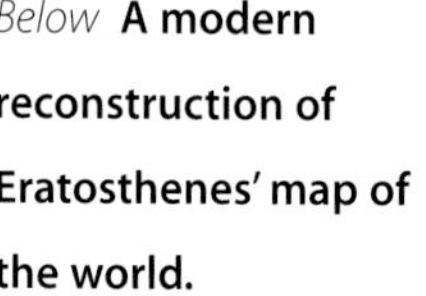

Below **A modern reconstruction of Eratosthenes' map of the world.**

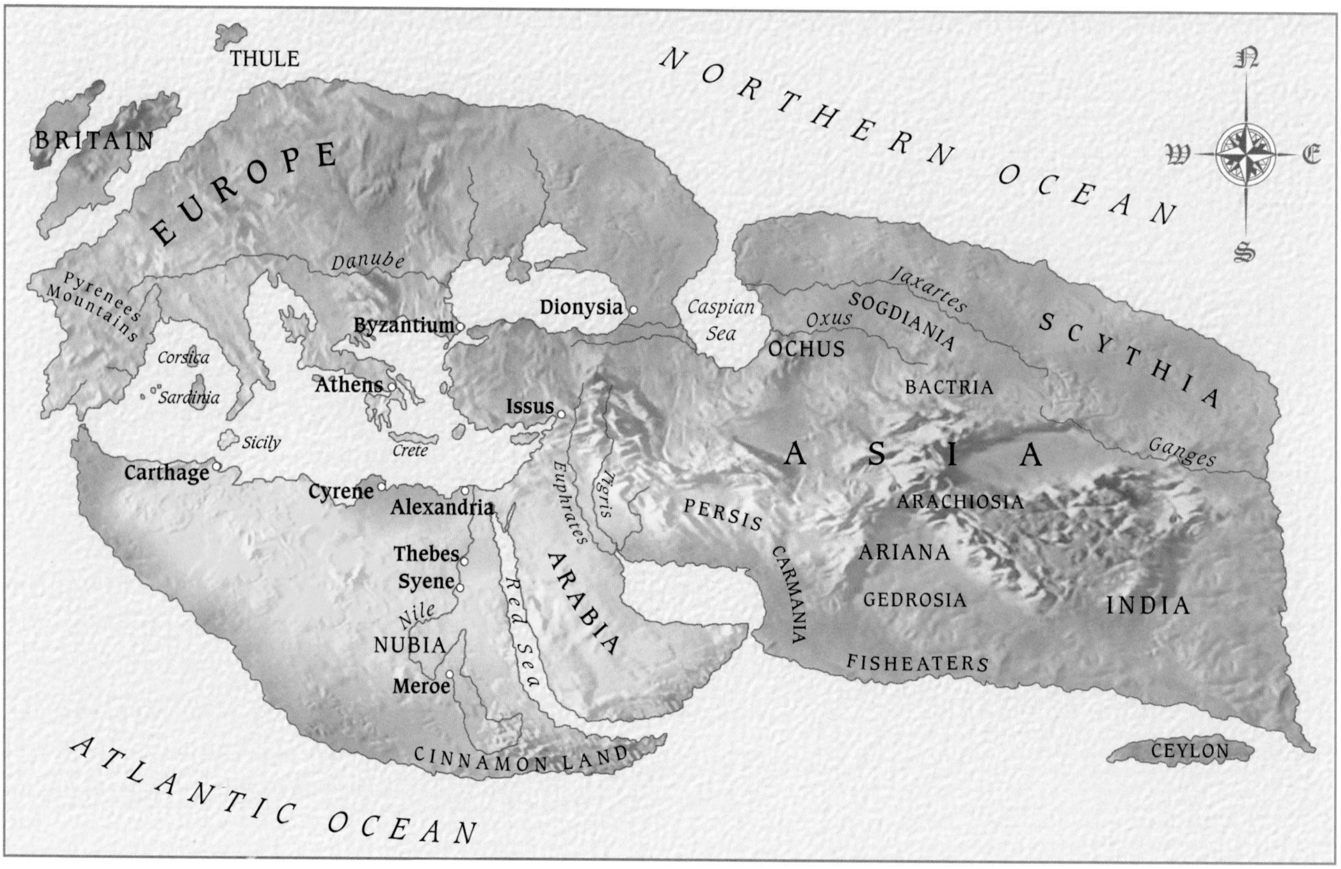

Eratosthenes' map marks a significant milestone in the history of cartography (the science and art of mapmaking). He was the first cartographer to plot the exact positions of physical features on a grid of parallel lines—a system that remains the standard method of positioning objects on a map. As a baseline for his grid, Eratosthenes used a line running from Gibraltar (at the southern tip of Spain) in the west to the Himalayas in the east. This choice was another first, since all earlier Greek maps had been centered on the Greek town of Delphi, which was thought of as the center, or navel, of the world.

A Sea Passage to India

Eratosthenes' *Geographica* is now lost, but in the writings of Strabo (c. 64 BCE–c. 21 CE), the ancient world's leading writer on geography, a tantalizing glimpse of the genius of Eratosthenes is preserved. Strabo quotes Eratosthenes as saying, "If the extent of the Atlantic Ocean were not an obstacle, we might easily pass by sea from Iberia (Spain) to India, keeping in the same parallel." This passage suggests that, as long ago as the third century BCE, the ancient Greeks believed that a sea passage to India might be found by sailing westward across the Atlantic Ocean. It was precisely this belief that led Columbus to make his famous voyage to the West Indies centuries later, in 1492.

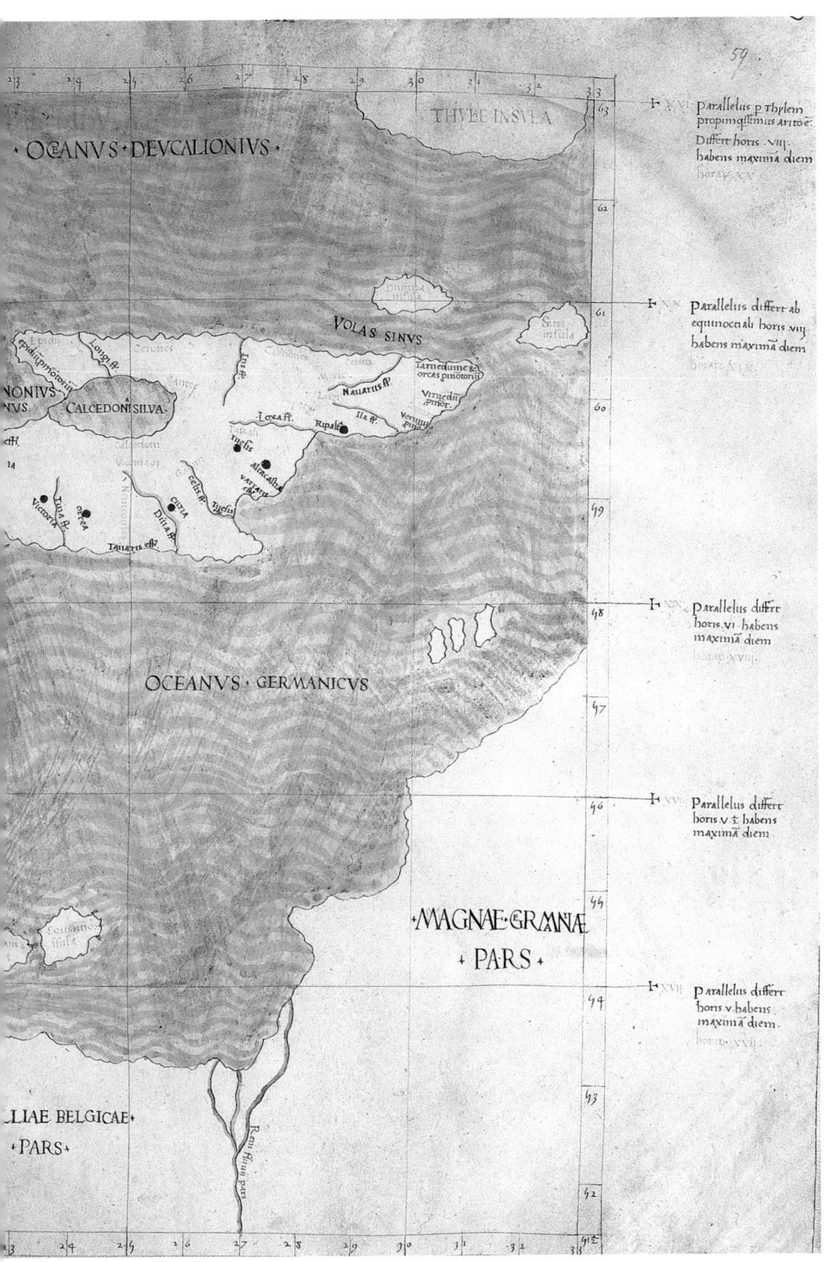

Eratosthenes was also the first geographer to propose a map projection—a method of representing the spherical earth on a flat surface that took into account the curvature of the planet.

Left **This fifteenth-century map is based on Ptolemy's second-century description of the British Isles. The map includes the land of Thule (pictured at upper right, to the northeast of Scotland), a land also described in Eratosthenes' *Geographica*. The first reports of Thule came from Pytheas, who, from his hometown of Massalia (present-day Marseilles in southern France), explored the Atlantic coast of Europe during the third century BCE. Pytheas considered Thule to be the northernmost inhabited island; it lay six days' sail from northern Britain and extended at least to the Arctic Circle. The region Pytheas visited is probably part of present-day Iceland or Norway.**

SEE ALSO

- Alexander the Great
- Columbus, Christopher
- Geography
- Map Projection
- Strabo

Erik the Red

ERIK THE RED (also known as Erik Thorvaldson), who lived in the latter part of the tenth century CE, is remembered variously as an explorer, a colonist, a murderer, and an outlaw. The first European to explore Greenland, he gave that country its name and established colonies there for settlers from Iceland. He was the father of Freydis Eriksdottir and Leif, Thorstein, and Thorvald Eriksson, renowned Norse explorers and settlers of North America.

Outlaw

According to Norse sagas, Erik was born in about 950 at Jaeder in southwestern Norway. As a son of Thorvald Aswaldsson, he was named Erik Thorvaldson, though his red hair led to his more familiar nickname, Erik the Red. After some form of conflict, he and his father were forced to leave Norway and sailed to Iceland, four hundred miles (645 km) northwest of Jaeder, where they set up home.

Right **This Norse ship, carved on limestone during the eighth or ninth century CE, is the type of vessel that was used by Erik the Red and his fellow Viking explorers as they traveled the northern Atlantic.**

c. 950
Erik the Red is born at Jaeder, Norway.

c. 950s
As a young boy, is taken to Iceland by his father.

c. 982
Is banished from Iceland for three years; sails west and settles at Eriksfjord, near the southwestern tip of Greenland.

c. 982–985
Explores the west coast of Greenland.

c. 985–986
Returns to Iceland; leads colonizing expedition to southwestern Greenland.

c. 986–1000
The western, middle, and eastern settlements are established in Greenland.

c. 1003
Erik dies in Greenland.

Following his father's death, Erik married and moved to western Iceland, where he built a farm. Then, in about 981, he killed two of his fellow settlers in a quarrel and moved to another location—where he killed two more settlers. As punishment Erik was outlawed and banished from Iceland for three years. Because of the events of his childhood, he was unable to return to Norway, and so he looked to the west.

A thirteenth-century account of Erik's exploration and settlement of Greenland:

Erik headed south, to discover whether the land was habitable. He spent his first winter at Eriksey . . . and the following spring went on to Eriksfjord where he sited his house. . . . During the third summer he pressed on north . . . [then] turned back and spent the third winter at Eriksey. . . . The following summer he returned to Iceland and . . . [then] went off to colonize that land he had discovered, calling it Greenland, for he argued that men would be all the more drawn to go there if the land had an attractive name.

Saga of Erik the Red

Erik Sails Westward

With his wife and children, Erik joined a voyage westward from Iceland in 982. Erik knew that fifty years earlier land had been-sighted in the west. The *Saga of Erik the Red* records that he planned to "look for that land Gunnbjörn Ulf-Krakason sighted the time he was storm-driven west across the ocean."

After a 175-mile (280 km) voyage, Erik and his crew reached a part of the east coast of Greenland named Gunnbjörn's Skerries after the man who had first set eyes on it. They landed near a glacier, but as the area was too icy for settlement, they moved south along the coast. Erik built a farm at Eriksfjord and spent the next three years exploring the west coast of Greenland.

Greenland Is Colonized

Sometime around 985 Erik returned to Iceland, where he ran into trouble once again. He decided to leave Iceland for good and establish a colony in the land he had explored. He gave the new country the name Greenland, in the hope that this name would encourage more people to colonize it. His plan succeeded, partly because of widespread famine in Iceland, and in 986 around eight hundred would-be colonists sailed from Iceland in twenty-five ships. Only fourteen reached Greenland. Of the others some were wrecked, and some turned back.

Below **The route taken by the Vikings from Norway via the Shetlands to Iceland and Greenland in the ninth and tenth centuries.**

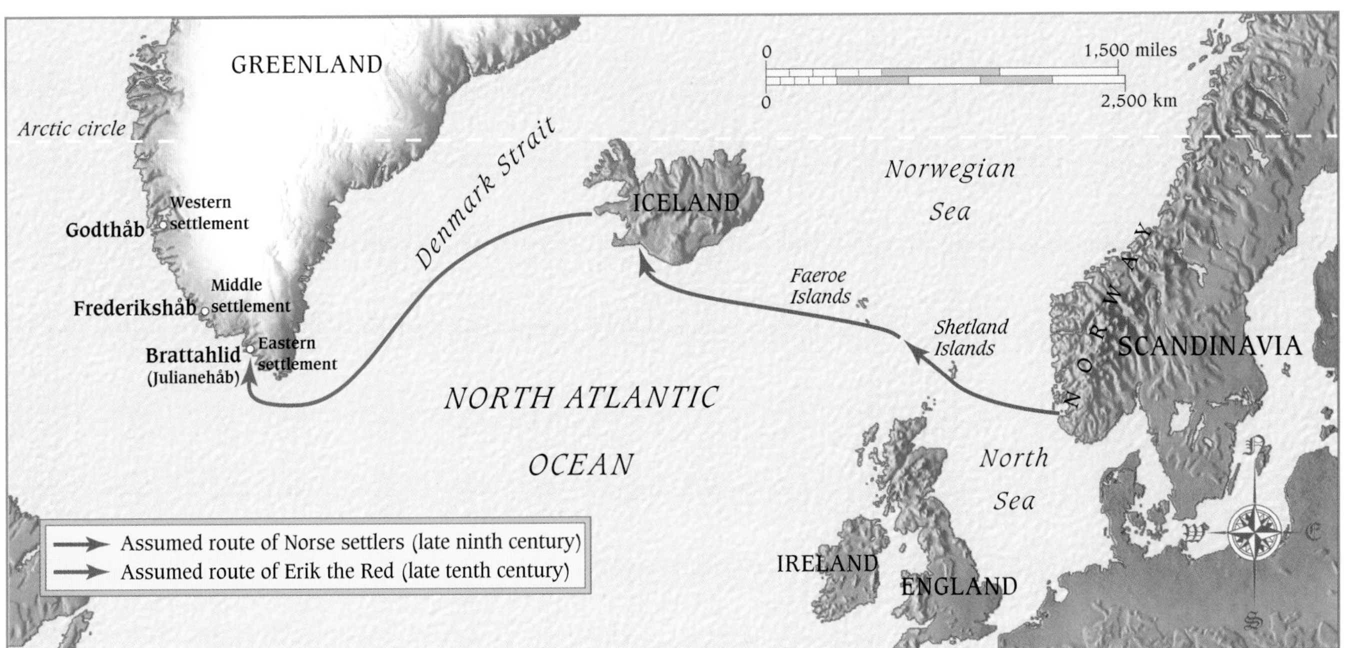

Right **Remains of Norse buildings at Brattahlid, the site of Erik's farm in the eastern settlement in Greenland.**

Norse Seafarers

Between the eighth and eleventh centuries the North Atlantic was the domain of Norse (or Viking) seafarers from Norway, Sweden, and Denmark. In the 700s the Norse began a period of colonization, driven by the need to find new land to farm. Sailing westward across the North Sea, in the early ninth century Norse settlers established communities on Orkney and Shetland (island groups north of Britain). By 860 the Norse had reached the Faeroe Islands, and during the late ninth century Iceland was settled. Each new landing point served as a stepping stone for further voyages.

About five hundred colonists arrived at the southwestern tip of Greenland and settled down to a farming life. Erik built his farm, Brattahlid, on Greenland's most fertile fjord. It was part of a scattered community of around 190 farms that came to be known as the eastern settlement (the area surrounds present-day Qassiarsuk, or Julianehåb). A second, smaller settlement (the middle settlement) had around twenty farms and was established at present-day Frederikshåb (Paamiut), and a third, the western settlement, consisted of around ninety farms and was centered farther north around the present-day capital of Godthåb (Nuuk).

Decline of the Colonies

Erik died in about 1003. The Greenland colonies survived for five hundred years after his death. However, during the fourteenth century the colonies lost contact with Iceland and Norway and began to decline. At the same time the climate cooled, with disastrous consequences. Greenland's ice sheet spread, and storms raged in the North Atlantic. A fall in the production of crops and livestock led to starvation among the colonists. The cold temperatures also caused the native Inuit to travel farther south than was usual, and there were conflicts with the settlers. By 1500 the three settlements had died out.

SEE ALSO

- Gudrid
- Leif Eriksson
- Vikings

EXPLORATION AND GEOGRAPHICAL SOCIETIES

DURING THE NINETEENTH CENTURY geographical societies played a major role in sponsoring journeys of exploration and in making the public aware of new discoveries. These societies continue to fund expeditions and field research and to increase knowledge of the world through their publications and their educational projects.

Below **As president of the Royal Society of London for over forty years, the botanist Joseph Banks, the subject of this 1773 portrait, was chief scientific adviser to the British government.**

ROYAL SOCIETY

The origins of geographical societies lie in the seventeenth century, when a scientific revolution was taking place in Europe. At the forefront was the Royal Society of London. Formally established in 1660, the Royal Society is the oldest scientific body in existence. The first scientific organization to support voyages of exploration, it was the forerunner of geographical societies. One of its many achievements was to encourage government-sponsored voyages of exploration to include scientists among their crew.

THE AFRICAN ASSOCIATION

The first society devoted solely to geography was the African Association, set up in London in 1788 by Sir Joseph Banks, president of the Royal Society, and Henry Beaufoy, a politician. The African Associaton was a small but influential organization whose members, mostly noblemen, included three dukes and twelve earls. Its aim was to send expeditions to explore the African interior, which Beaufoy described as a "wide extended blank."

The explorers were instructed to trace the course of the great African rivers, such as the Niger and the Nile. Between 1788 and 1830 the association sent over a dozen explorers to Africa, the most famous of whom was Mungo Park, who died in 1806, probably ambushed while tracing the course of the Niger River.

Transits

In the 1760s the Royal Society sponsored dozens of expeditions to observe two rare astronomical events called transits. Transits take place when planets move into line between the earth and the sun and thus can be seen as shadows moving across the face of the sun.

In 1716 the astronomer Edmund Halley predicted that two transits of Venus would occur in close succession, in 1761 and 1769. Halley proposed sending out expeditions to many distant parts of the earth to observe and time the transits. The information they gathered could then be used to work out the distance between the earth and the sun.

The best known of these expeditions was that of Captain James Cook. From the island of Tahiti in the Pacific, Cook observed the 1769 transit of Venus. Later the same year, from a vantage point in New Zealand, Cook also observed the transit of Mercury.

The African Association was driven by the thirst for scientific knowledge. The founders also hoped to convert Africans to Christianity and to find new markets for British goods. Beaufoy, a leading member of the Society for the Abolition of Slavery, hoped to end the African slave trade.

French Prizes

The oldest geographical society still in existence is the French Societé de Géographie de Paris, founded in 1821. The society offered prizes of money and medals for feats of exploration. In 1824 it announced a prize of ten thousand francs to the first European to find and report back on Tombouctou (Timbuktu), a city in West Africa rumored in Europe to have buildings roofed with gold. The prize was won by René Caillié, who traveled to the city in 1828 disguised as an Egyptian Muslim. Disappointed by what he found, Caillié described Tombouctou as a "mass of ill-looking houses built of earth."

German Scientists

It was in Germany that geography became a science in its own right, largely because of the work of three men: the scientific explorer Alexander von Humboldt (1769–1859), the mathematician and mapmaker Heinrich

Right **Carl Ritter (1779–1859), a founder of the German Geographical Society, planned to write a complete geographical description of the world. By the time of his death, he had finished nineteen volumes but only got as far as Asia and Africa.**

1660
Royal Society is formally established in London.

1768–1769
Captain James Cook makes his first voyage to the Pacific.

1788
African Association is founded.

1821
Societé de Géographie is founded in Paris.

1828
René Caillié reaches Tombouctou.
Gesellschaft für Erdkunde (Society for Earth Sciences) is founded in Berlin.

1830
Royal Geographical Society (RGS) is founded in London.

1838
First geographical society in the Americas is founded in Rio de Janeiro, Brazil.

1845
Russian Geographical Society is founded in Saint Petersburg.

1845–1862
Alexander von Humboldt's *Kosmos* is published.

1848–1860
RGS helps send expeditions in search of Sir John Franklin, lost in the Canadian Arctic.

1852
The American Geographical Society is set up in New York.

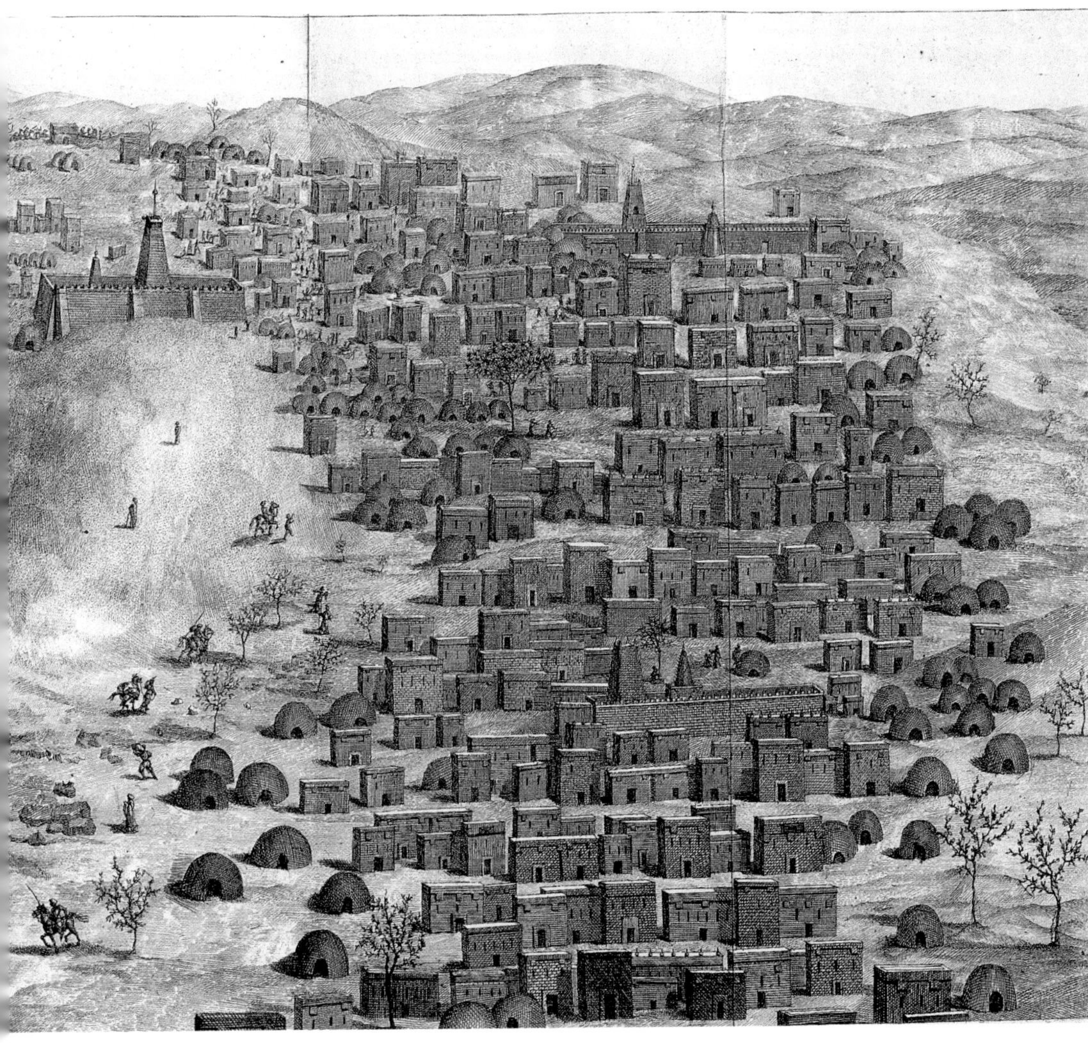

Above **In his *Journal d'un voyage à Temboctou* (1830), from which this engraving is taken, René Caillié put paid to rumors of a fabulously wealthy city.**

Berghaus (1797–1884), and the geographer Carl Ritter (1779–1859).

Alexander von Humboldt has been called the greatest scientific traveler who ever lived. Between 1799 and 1804 he explored six thousand miles (9,600 km) of territory in South America and collected data on geology, botany, peoples, ocean currents, climate, and the magnetism of the earth. To Humboldt all these aspects of nature were interrelated. In 1834 he wrote that he had "the crazy notion to depict in a single work the entire material universe, all that we know of the phenomena of heaven and earth."

1853–1856
David Livingstone makes first crossing of Africa.

1857–1858
Burton and Speke search for the source of the Nile.

1871
First International Geographical Congress is held in Antwerp.

1888
National Geographic Society is founded in Washington, DC.

1901–1904
Robert Scott's first Antarctic expedition is funded with money raised by the Royal Geographical Society.

1904
Association of American Geographers is founded in Philadelphia.

1909
Robert Peary launches an expedition to the North Pole.

1922
International Geographical Union is formed.

1929
Royal Canadian Geographical Society is founded.

1953
Edmund Hillary and Tenzing Norgay, sponsored by the RGS and the Alpine Club, climb Everest, the highest mountain on earth.

1997
Eleven European geographical societies combine to form the European Geographical Society (EUGEO).

Humboldt made Berlin a center for the study of geography. It was there that, in 1828, Heinrich Berghaus and Carl Ritter founded the Gesellschaft für Erdkunde (Society for Earth Sciences), the second of the national geographical societies. This society would spread Humboldt's ideas and influence many later scientific explorers.

Royal Geographical Society

In 1826 in London, a group of forty rich travelers joined together to form the Raleigh Travellers' Club. The idea was that every fortnight the members would each in turn provide a banquet, featuring specialities from the land he had most recently visited. At the first Raleigh Travellers' Club dinner, members enjoyed a feast of reindeer meat from Spitsbergen (a group of islands in the North Sea off the coast of Norway) and berries from Lapland (an area of northern Scandinavia), washed down with Swedish brandy.

One of the leading members of the Raleigh Club was Sir John Barrow. As secretary to the Admiralty, Barrow was already sending out naval officers on expeditions of exploration. In 1828 he proposed that the Raleigh Club set up a new society to promote "that most important and entertaining branch of knowledge—geography." Two years later, on July 16, 1830, the Royal Geographical Society (RGS) was launched.

Right **The garden of the headquarters of the Royal Geographical Society (RGS) in Kensington, West London. Together with the Institute of British Geographers, the RGS publishes academic journals, organizes conferences and lectures, and provides grants for research and fieldwork. The RGS has 13,000 members, and its map room houses over two million maps, atlases, books, and photographs.**

The RGS played a leading role in nineteenth- and twentieth-century exploration. In 1831 the RGS absorbed the African Association and continued its project of tracing Africa's great rivers. Among the society's explorers were David Livingstone, Richard Burton, and John Hanning Speke.

In the 1890s the RGS promoted the exploration of Antarctica. The quest for the South Pole preoccupied Sir Clement Markham (president of the RGS from 1893 to 1905). Markham organized the National Antarctic Expedition (1901–1904) and launched the career of Captain Robert Scott, who commanded the expedition and became one of the world's most famous polar explorers.

The Polar Controversy

One important role of the RGS and other geographical societies is to provide a venue for returning explorers to present their findings. In 1909, for example, two U.S. explorers, Frederick Cook and Robert Peary, each claimed to have reached the North Pole. Cook was unmasked as a fraud when photographs he said he had taken at the Pole were shown to be cropped versions of photos taken years earlier in Greenland. Peary then submitted his proof—observations of the sun at midday—to the U.S. National Geographic Society, which along with the RGS, concluded that Peary was an honorable man who would not fake records. The RGS awarded Peary a gold medal, an honor accorded only to the greatest explorers. Other geographical societies followed this lead, and Peary was showered with medals.

In 1989 the National Geographic Society asked experts to reexamine Peary's evidence, including previously unpublished photos. The experts concluded that he must have got to within five miles of the Pole. However, two more recent Arctic explorers, Wally Herbert and Ranulph Fiennes, have argued that Peary could not have traveled the distance he claimed in the time available to him. Though their claims have as many detractors as supporters, the Peary controversy continues.

Berghaus's Atlas

Heinrich Berghaus (1797–1884) not only founded the German Geographical Society, he later produced one of the very first thematic atlases—a book of maps organized according to different themes. Published in 1837 and 1838, Berghaus's *Physikalischer Atlas* was a beautifully illustrated collection of ninety-three maps. Its themes included climate, geology, the magnetism of the earth, and the distribution of plants, animals, and peoples. Berghaus's atlas was inspired by the work of the German scientist and explorer Alexander von Humboldt and recorded many of his discoveries.

Right **Machu Picchu, a lost Incan city high in the Peruvian Andes Mountains, was rediscovered in 1911 by Hiram Bingham, an explorer sent by the U.S. National Geographic Society.**

Worldwide Societies

By the early 1900s there were over a hundred geographical societies around the world, including three in the United States, the most famous being the National Geographic Society, founded in 1888 in Washington, DC. Although chiefly known for its magazine, *National Geographic*, the society has also helped fund thousands of expeditions. The National Geographic Society sponsored the explorer Hiram Bingham, who discovered the lost Inca city of Machu Picchu in Peru in 1911.

Throughout the twentieth century, more geographical societies were set up, the most recent being the European Geographical Society (EUGEO) in 1997. The central aim of EUGEO is to "raise and stimulate awareness of geography and environmental matters." Thanks largely to the work of geographical societies, far more is known about the earth now than was known by the founders of the African Association in 1788. Geographical societies play a vital role by focusing people's attention on the threats to the environment caused by the loss of forests, climate change, and pollution.

In his autobiography the scientist Francis Galton described how, in 1849, he had vague ambitions to become an explorer of Africa but had no idea how to go about it:

My cousin . . . suggested my putting myself in communication with the Royal Geographical Society, where I could learn precisely whereabouts exploration was especially desirable, and where I should be sure to receive influential support. He offered introductions to some of its leading members, which I gladly accepted. . . . The immediate helpfulness to a traveler of such a Society is very great. . . . My vague plans were now carefully discussed, made more definite, and approved.

Francis Galton, *Memories of My Life*

SEE ALSO

- Burton, Richard Francis • Cook, James
- Flinders, Matthew • France • Geography
- Humboldt, Alexander von • Livingstone, David
- Park, Mungo • Peary, Robert E.
- Scott, Robert Falcon • Speke, John Hanning
- Stanley, Henry Morton

FAXIAN

FAXIAN, ALSO KNOWN AS Fa-hsien, was born in the valley of the Yellow River in Shanxi Province, China, during the fourth century CE. Orphaned at an early age, he became a Buddhist monk and in 399 undertook an epic pilgrimage to India, the Buddhist holy land. Journeying overland, he visited numerous religious sites in northern India before returning by sea via Sri Lanka. Back home he continued his scholarly work until his death around 465. Although primarily a pilgrim, the records Faxian kept of his remarkable travels mark him out as a true explorer.

Above **The remote and beautiful Mount Wutai, a site sacred to Buddhists, is situated in Shanxi Province, the birthplace of Faxian.**

ACROSS THE DESERTS

Faxian was originally named Sehi, but as an adult he changed his name for religious reasons to Faxian, which means "splendor of religious law." Before Faxian's father died, he had planned a religious career for his son. The boy rejected other offers and chose to follow the path laid out for him. At a young age he became a novice in a Buddhist monastery. The Buddhist religion, which had begun in India around 500 BCE, was closely associated with education and was flourishing in China at this time.

c. 399
Faxian sets out on pilgrimage to India.

c. 402
Reaches northwestern India.

c. 411
Travels to Ceylon (Sri Lanka).

c. 413
Sets sail for China.

c. 414
Arrives home.

c. 465
Dies.

Legend reports that Faxian soon became known for his piety and scholarship. According to one story, he was such a good talker that he persuaded thieves not to rob his monastery's grain store. By the time he was in his twenties, Faxian was increasingly vexed that, as a result of living in China, he had received his faith secondhand and that he was unfamiliar with India, the spiritual homeland of the Buddhist religion. Faxian decided therefore to make a pilgrimage to India. He set out on a journey on which he would eventually cover several thousand miles.

From Sian (Chang'an), Faxian traveled west across the trackless wastes of central Asia that lay between the Gobi Desert, the Kunlun Mountains, and the Tien Shan Mountains. The landscape was bleak beyond his imagining. Tormented by thirst, hunger, and cold and threatened by robbers and brigands, on several occasions Faxian came close to death. However, surviving his ordeals, he finally reached Khotan and then turned to the south and traveled across the Karakoram Mountains to the Indus River, which flows through northwestern India and present-day Pakistan.

Below **This map shows Faxian's route through South and Southeast Asia (399–414).**

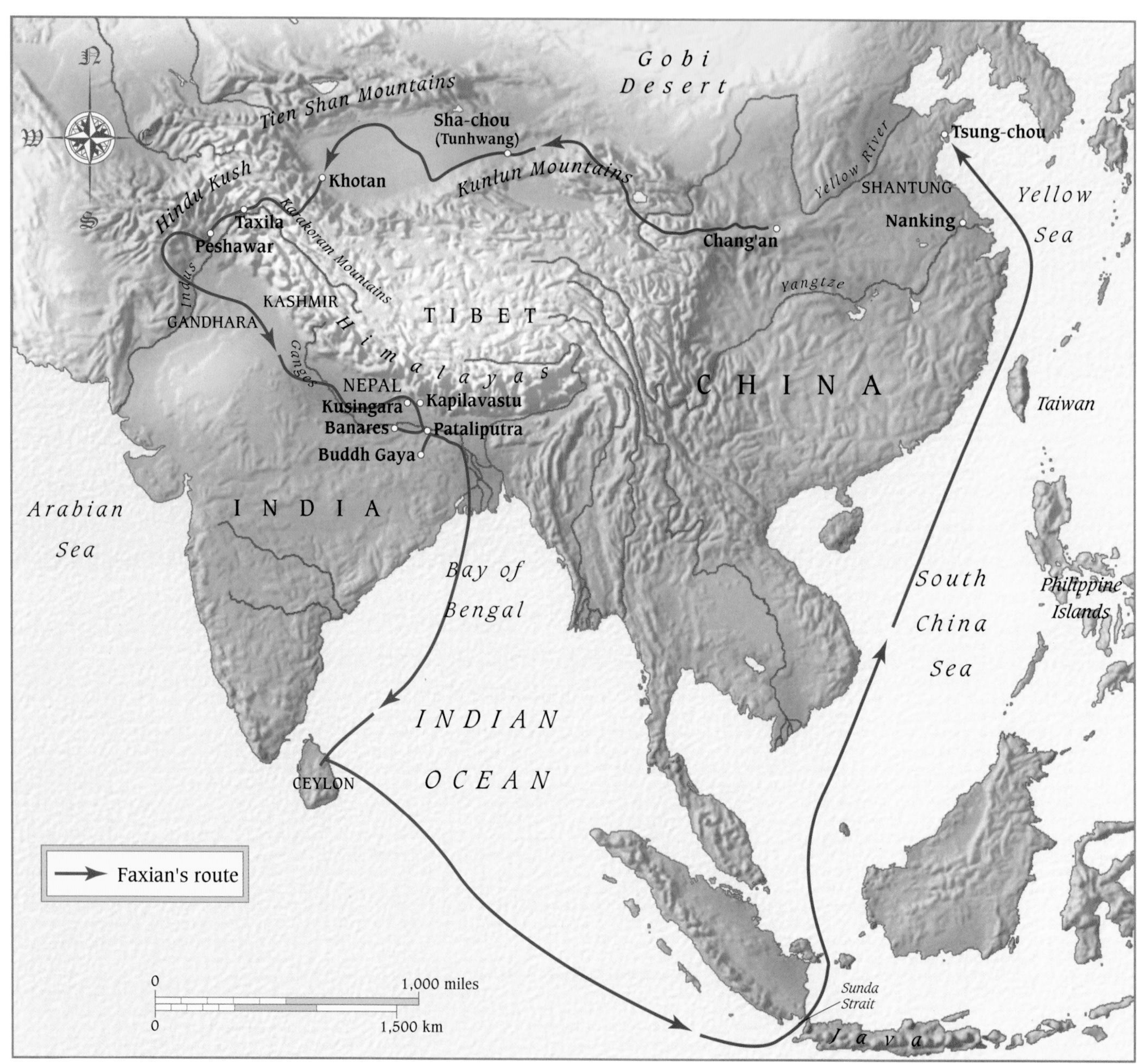

Holy Land

India was rich and peaceful, and everywhere Faxian went, he found Buddhism flourishing. Over several years he visited Gandhara, Taxila, Udyana, and Peshawar, the great seats of learning in the northwest, where he studied ancient texts in the Sanskrit language and talked with a large number of other scholars and holy men.

Faxian then crossed to eastern India and toured the four holiest Buddhist sites. The first of these was Kapilavastu, the birthplace of Prince Gautama Siddhartha (c. 563–483 BCE), the founder of Buddhism. The second holy site was Buddh Gaya, where the prince had received enlightenment and thus become the Buddha, or "enlightened one." The third was Benares (present-day Varanasi), where the Buddha had first preached. Finally, at Kusinagara (present-day Kasia) Faxian visited the place where the Buddha had died and was presumed to enter nirvana, the Buddhist afterlife.

The Journey Home

In all the places he visited, Faxian talked with fellow monks. He also collected and copied precious Sanskrit manuscripts, which were unknown in China, to take home for translation. Eventually, feeling it was his duty to pass on the knowledge he had acquired to his fellow countrymen and women, Faxian left for home.

After the troubles of his overland route, Faxian decided to make the journey homeward by ship. Unfortunately, the return journey was just as dangerous as the outward one had been. A two-year stay in Ceylon (present-day Sri Lanka) was followed by two hundred perilous days at sea. Faxian's ship ran into two huge storms. The first storm drove the ship to an unknown island, perhaps Java (the most populous island of Indonesia). The second storm again threatened shipwreck and carried the vessel many miles off course. By the time the ship approached Shantung in northern China, the crew had lost all sense of direction and had no idea where it was. It was Faxian who recognized the local vegetation and realized they must be almost home at last.

> Faxian describes the arid wastes of central Asia that he had to cross to reach India:
>
> *In the desert were numerous evil spirits and scorching winds, causing death of anyone who would meet with them. Above there were no birds, while on the ground there were no animals. One looked as far as one could in all directions for a path to cross, but there was none to choose. Only the dried bones of the dead served as indicators.*
>
> Quoted in Kenneth K. S. Ch'en, *Buddhism in China: A Historical Survey*

Ambassador, Scholar, Explorer

It is difficult to overestimate Faxian's importance. He was largely responsible for opening formal relations between China and India. Chinese Buddhism was much strengthened by the sacred texts he brought back from India and Sri Lanka. His pilgrimage was the first recorded journey between China and India by land and sea. Finally, his *Fo Kuo Chi* (Record of Buddhistic kingdoms) is an invaluable historical document that gives modern scholars a clear insight into the Buddhist period of India's history, before Buddhist civilization was overwhelmed first by Hindu and later by Islamic civilizations.

SEE ALSO

- Cheng Ho
- Silk Road
- Zhang Heng

FERDINAND AND ISABELLA

Below **King Ferdinand V and his wife, Isabella I (right), with their eldest daughter, Juana, also known as Juana la Loca (Joan the Mad). When Isabella died in 1504, Ferdinand had Juana declared queen of Castile.**

THE MARRIAGE IN 1469 of Princess Isabella (1451–1504) of the kingdom of Castile and Prince Ferdinand II (1452–1516) of the kingdom of Aragon proved to be the most significant union of the Age of Discovery. When they were crowned head of their respective kingdoms, Castile and Aragon, the greater part of Spain was united under a single rule, and the foundations were laid for the unrivaled wealth and power of Spain in the sixteenth century. Perhaps the most crucial moment in the Age of Discovery was the Spanish decision to back the 1492 voyage of Christopher Columbus westward across the Atlantic, a voyage that led to Spain's acquisition of a vast overseas empire in the Americas.

THE CATHOLIC MONARCHS

Although Prince Ferdinand had many impressive qualities—he was brave, honest, and wise—he kept his emotions hidden behind a mask of coldness, and many found him unappealing. His marriage to Isabella, when she was only eighteen and he only seventeen, was a political act aimed at creating a powerful new dynasty. His young and deeply religious bride matched Ferdinand in intelligence. Despite the fact that their marriage was arranged, Ferdinand and Isabella grew to love each other and produced five children.

Isabella became queen of Castile in 1474, and Ferdinand king of Aragon and joint ruler of Castile (where he was styled Ferdinand V) five years later. Civil war filled the years between, as Ferdinand fought to get reluctant Castilians to accept his young wife's rule. Between 1482 and 1492 "their Catholic majesties," as the royal couple was known, were preoccupied with the *Reconquista*. When the city of Granada finally fell on January 2, 1492, Ferdinand and Isabella were free to pursue more momentous projects.

CHRISTOPHER COLUMBUS

The Italian sailor Christopher Columbus first tried to secure backing for a transatlantic voyage to the Indies (India and China) in 1484.

Left **Ferdinand and Isabella bidding farewell to Christopher Columbus on August 3, 1492. As with many other paintings, this one depicts an event that probably never happened.**

When he was turned down by King John II of Portugal, then Europe's leading nation of maritime exploration, Columbus turned to Spain. Ferdinand and Isabella took six years to consider his scheme. Finally, immediately after the fall of Granada, Isabella granted Columbus an audience and agreed to support his project.

Ferdinand's opinion of Columbus is not known; it seems that the key decision to back the voyage came from Isabella, who was guided more by her passionate Catholic faith than by a lust for empire or gold. She believed that the reconquest of Granada from the Muslims had been sanctioned by God and that the expansion of the Catholic kingdom of Spain westward would have the same sanction. In her eyes Columbus's enterprise was a religious crusade.

The *Reconquista*

In the early eighth century almost all of Spain was conquered by the Muslim Moors (people of mixed Spanish and Arab descent). The *Reconquista* (reconquest) was the eight-hundred-year struggle to drive out the Moors. The campaign was finally concluded in 1492, with Ferdinand and Isabella's capture of Granada, the last Muslim stronghold in Spain. Columbus was present at the fall of Granada, and the monarchs' backing for his westward expedition in the same year was, to some extent, a fresh expression of the spirit of *Reconquista*.

1451
Isabella is born.

1452
Ferdinand is born.

1469
Ferdinand and Isabella are married.

1474
Isabella becomes queen of Castile.

1479
Ferdinand becomes king of Aragon and joint monarch of Castile.

1484
Columbus tries to get backing from Portugal.

1492
Reconquista is complete as Granada falls; Ferdinand and Isabella back Columbus's first voyage.

1494
Pope divides unknown world between Spain and Portugal with Treaty of Tordesillas.

1504
Isabella dies.

1506
Columbus dies.

1516
Ferdinand dies.

Below **These ceramic tiles, made in 1929, show the reception of Columbus at the court of Ferdinand and Isabella in Barcelona in April 1493. The royal letter that invited "our Admiral of the Ocean Sea" to court told him to "come at once, and make haste!"**

One of the queen's confessors persuaded her to meet with Columbus, and a member of the Santa Hermandad (a kind of national police force established by the two monarchs) helped finance Columbus's first expedition. The story that Isabella offered her jewels as security for the enterprise is probably untrue. Nevertheless, Columbus named the settlement of La Isabela on the Caribbean island of Hispaniola in her honor.

The Problems of Empire

According to Columbus's agreement with Ferdinand and Isabella, any new lands discovered would be considered possessions of the Spanish crown and their inhabitants would be Spanish subjects. This crucial decision set the precedent for future exploration and enabled Spain to benefit enormously from an overseas empire entirely under its control. An alternative plan would have allowed nobles and other wealthy sponsors of expeditions to set up overseas power bases of their own—a sure recipe for chaos.

Columbus was appointed governor of the territories he discovered. It was soon clear, however, that Isabella and her explorer had quite different ideas of what good governorship meant. The central issue was the treatment of the native inhabitants, who became known as Indians (Columbus never gave up the belief that he had reached Asia).

Columbus treated the Indians under his rule harshly. The queen, on the other hand, urged kindness and even set free some of the Indian slaves Columbus brought to Spain.

A Lasting Legacy

Greeted as a hero on his return from his first voyage in 1493, Columbus gradually fell from royal favor during his subsequent expeditions (1493–1496, 1498–1500, and 1502–1504). Indeed, it is likely that the monarchs backed his fourth voyage more in pity than hope. After the death of Isabella in 1504, Columbus spent the remaining months of his life trying in vain to get Ferdinand to grant him the rewards he believed were still owed him.

The rush of exploration and New World conquest that followed Columbus's expeditions was more than any king could control closely. Besides, much of Ferdinand's time was taken up with domestic and European matters. Nevertheless, he and his councillors successfully maintained the principles already established by Isabella and himself.

Part of Columbus's agreement with Ferdinand and Isabella:

Your Highnesses, as Catholic Christians, and princes who love and promote the holy Christian faith . . . determined to send me, Christopher Columbus, to the above-mentioned countries of India . . . and furthermore directed that I should not proceed by land to the East, as is customary, but by a Westerly route, in which direction we have hitherto no certain evidence that any one has gone . . . and for that purpose granted me great favors, and ennobled me that thenceforth I might call myself Don, and be High Admiral of the Sea . . .

Columbus's Journal (1492)

Above **This wood engraving shows Ferdinand and Isabella entering the captured Muslim province of Granada, in southern Spain, in 1492. Backing for Columbus's voyage was an offshoot of Spain's national optimism in the wake of the *Reconquista*.**

All exploration in the territory granted to Spain by the Treaty of Tordesillas (1494) had to be authorized by the crown, and all newly acquired land belonged to the crown. Thus, royal authority had some control over Spain's exploration and settlement of the Americas. Although the process was marked by acts of cruelty, in less competent hands things might well have been worse. Indeed, had Isabella and Ferdinand not had the imagination and courage to back Columbus in the first place, the history of New World exploration might have been very different.

SEE ALSO

• Columbus, Christopher • Spain

Fitzroy, Robert

ROBERT FITZROY (1805–1865), A DISTINGUISHED OFFICER in the Royal Navy, took command of HMS *Beagle* in 1828, when the ship's captain committed suicide. In 1831 the young Charles Darwin accompanied Fitzroy on a five-year voyage to the Pacific coast of South America. After a brief career in politics, Fitzroy worked to develop the new science of meteorology, and in 1854 he became the first head of the British Meteorological Office. In later years Fitzroy felt increasingly responsible for Darwin's theory of evolution, which challenged the traditional Christian view, held by Fitzroy himself, of the creation of the world. He took his own life in 1865.

Below **A great-grandson of King Charles II, Robert Fitzroy felt that he was born to command.**

Voyage to South America

Robert Fitzroy, born into a wealthy aristocratic family, was marked out at an early age for a career as an officer in the Royal Navy. He graduated from the Royal Naval College in Portsmouth at the age of fourteen and was commissioned as an officer in 1824. Between 1826 and 1830 Fitzroy took his first major sea voyage, an expedition to survey the coast of South America.

The *Beagle,* captained by Pringle Stokes, and the *Adventure*, captained by Philip Parker King, set sail for South America with orders to survey the coastal waters around Patagonia and Tierra del Fuego (in present-day Argentina and Chile). The seas around Cape Horn, at the southern tip of the Americas, were especially dangerous, and few good sea charts of this area existed. After many months at sea, Stokes became depressed, and he committed suicide in August 1828. Fitzroy

1805
Robert Fitzroy is born at Ampton Hall, Suffolk.

1819
Enters the Royal Navy.

1824
Is commissioned as an officer in the Royal Navy.

1826–1830
Surveys coasts of South America.

1831–1836
HMS *Beagle* voyages to South America and across the Pacific.

1839
Fitzroy publishes his account of the voyage.

1841
Is elected member of Parliament for Durham.

1843
Is appointed governor of New Zealand.

1854
Becomes first head of the British Meteorological Office.

1860
Attends the infamous Oxford debate on evolution.

1863
Publishes *The Weather Book: A Manual of Practical Meteorology.*

1865
Commits suicide at Upper Norwood, near London.

took command of HMS *Beagle,* and the ship completed its mission and returned home to Britain in 1830. The success of the expedition demonstrated to the British authorities that Fitzroy was a trustworthy commander and an accurate mapmaker.

A Second Voyage on the *Beagle*

Soon afterward Fitzroy was ordered by the Admiralty to make a second scientific expedition to the Southern Hemisphere. He knew that, because of his aristocratic background and the traditions of the Royal Navy, he would have to remain aloof from the ordinary crewmen. Fearing months of loneliness, he decided to take with him the young naturalist Charles Darwin, who would collect specimens and act as a companion. Although there was little space in their cramped quarters, the men got on well with each other for most of the long voyage. Darwin found Fitzroy "open and kind," but the captain had a quick temper, and the two men quarreled over the issue of slavery.

The Surveying Corps

During the Napoleonic wars, fought between Britain and France from 1793 to 1815, it became clear to the Royal Navy that British sea charts were often roughly drawn and inaccurate. Large stretches of coastline around the world still remained unmapped. In 1817 the Admiralty set up a Corps of Surveying Officers under the command of Captain Thomas Hurd to improve the charts. Among the six survey ships built to undertake a series of long-distance mapping expeditions was HMS *Beagle*, launched in May 1820. It proved difficult to find officers willing to join the surveying corps. The work was very technical and needed great care and precision, and few naval officers had the necessary skills in cartography and mathematics. The survey ships were also away from home for many years at a time, a situation that put the men on board under great stress.

Below **HMS *Beagle* pictured in Jemmy Button Sound, Tierra del Fuego; the sound was named after the native boy that Fitzroy bought in exchange for a pearl button on his first voyage to the Americas.**

Below **Fitzroy sketched these natives of Tierra del Fuego on his second visit there in 1832. He tried to set up a mission to help advance the civilization of the Fuegians, but they preferred their traditional life of hunting and fishing.**

Fitzroy's surveying expedition to the Pacific, which lasted from 1831 to 1836, was considered a great success. The mission produced a wealth of maps and statistical information about the treacherous waters around Patagonia and the Strait of Magellan. Fitzroy also demonstrated that measurements of wind on the Beaufort Wind Scale and of air pressure (using barometers) could be used to forecast the weather at sea.

During the five-year around-the-world voyage, Fitzroy used his ship's chronometer to measure the ship's longitude (its position east or west of the Greenwich meridian). The data he collected were invaluable to later mapmakers, a fact that convinced the Admiralty to train all of its officers in this method of navigation. For his contribution Fitzroy was awarded the gold medal of the Royal Geographical Society in 1837. He published a three-volume account of the *Beagle*'s voyage in 1839. The third volume was written by Darwin, who described the flora and fauna he had observed.

Politician and Weatherman

Fitzroy was elected the member of Parliament for Durham in 1841, and two years later he was appointed governor of the new British colony of New Zealand. His governorship ended abruptly in 1845, when, after a rebellion in the north of the country, British settlers complained to London that Fitzroy was too sympathetic to the grievances of the native Maori people.

Fitzroy left the Royal Navy in 1850 with the rank of admiral and returned to his earlier studies of the weather. He was the first person to try to predict future weather by collecting information about the rise and fall in air pressure. He designed an improved stormglass (barometer), which was mass-produced after his death and named Admiral Fitzroy's Barometer.

Final Years

In the latter part of his life, Fitzroy became troubled by the part he had played in Charles Darwin's development of the theory of evolution, which conflicted with his own Christian beliefs. Fitzroy blamed himself for carrying Darwin to the Southern Hemisphere, where the naturalist's views had first taken shape. In 1860 Fitzroy attended a heated public debate on Darwin's theory of evolution at Oxford, during which he verbally attacked the biologist T. H. Huxley. Pointing to his copy of the Bible, Fitzroy declared, "Here is the truth—in here!"

When his weather-forecasting methods were ridiculed in the press, Fitzroy became deeply depressed. In 1865 he took his own life at his home near London. In 2002 an area of the North Atlantic previously named Finisterre was renamed Fitzroy in his honor.

SEE ALSO

• Chronometer • Darwin, Charles

The Father of British Meteorology

In 1854 Robert Fitzroy was appointed head of a new government department that became the British Meteorological Office. Its original purpose was simply to collect information about wind speed that might be useful to the Royal Navy. However, Fitzroy was a very energetic leader and the "Met Office" was soon observing and recording all aspects of the weather.

Fitzroy built a chain of barometer stations along the British coast to monitor air pressure. Their recordings were plotted in lines onto a map called a synoptic chart. This information allowed Fitzroy to forecast the likely weather in the coming days. He was also quick to appreciate that weather information could be transmitted using the new telegraphic message network. In 1860 he persuaded the *Times* of London to print daily weather information and encouraged other newspapers to follow suit. Three years later Fitzroy published *The Weather Book*, one of the earliest books about weather forecasting.

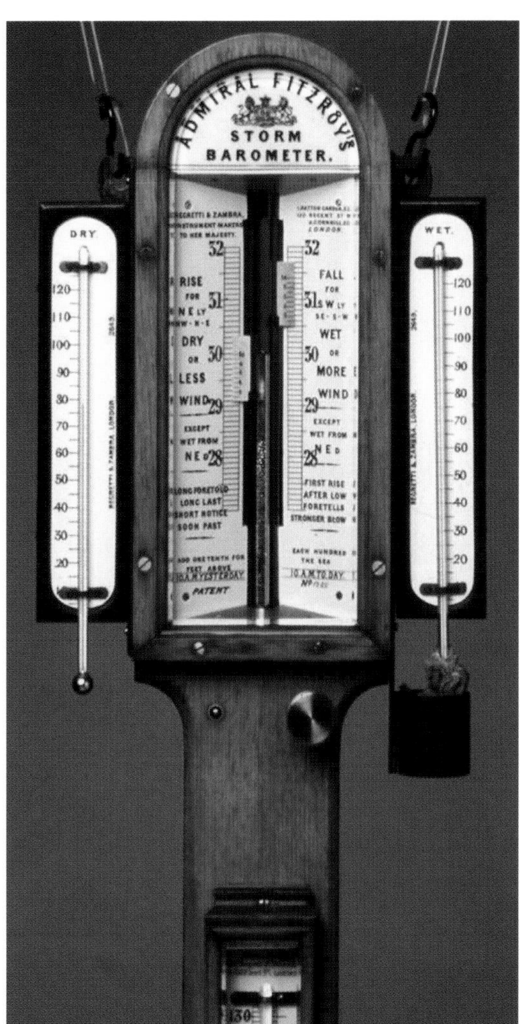

Left **Simple barometers had been used on board ships since the 1670s, but the Fitzroy barometer was a much more precise instrument. One special feature was Fitzroy's Remarks, comments that helped the sailor to understand the readings on the barometer and thus to predict the weather.**

FLINDERS, MATTHEW

AS A BRITISH NAVAL OFFICER Matthew Flinders (1774–1814) surveyed the coast of Australia. In the early nineteenth century, having become the first person to circumnavigate that continent, he was also the first to suggest that its name be changed from New Holland.

CHILDHOOD AMBITION

Matthew Flinders was born in 1774 in the village of Donington, eastern England. As a boy he read Daniel Defoe's *Robinson Crusoe*, a hugely popular seafaring story published in 1719. Flinders was inspired to become a sailor, and in 1789, at the age of fifteen, he joined the Royal Navy. Two years later he served as a midshipman on a voyage to the Pacific.

Right **In this 1801 portrait, Matthew Flinders wears the uniform of a British naval officer.**

VOYAGE TO NEW HOLLAND

Flinders's connection with Australia dates to 1795, when the country was known as New Holland. In that year he sailed to Port Jackson (present-day Sydney), where there was a colony of British prisoners. Traveling in a small boat, Flinders and two companions explored the surrounding coast. This expedition suggested to the governor of the colony that Flinders might be a suitable explorer of the country as a whole, and he encouraged Flinders to pursue his interest.

For the next three years Flinders charted the coast off southeastern Australia on the *Reliance*. In 1798, by sailing all the way around Van Diemen's Land (present-day Tasmania) with George Bass, he proved it was an island.

Flinders returned to England in 1800 and immediately began a campaign to gain support for an expedition to chart the entire coast of Australia. The British government, impressed with Flinders's achievements up to

1774
Matthew Flinders is born in Donington, eastern England.

1789
Joins the Royal Navy.

1791–1793
Sails to the Pacific with Captain Bligh.

1795–1796
Explores the region around Port Jackson (present-day Sydney) and the south coast of Australia.

1798–1799
Circumnavigates Van Diemen's Land.

1801–1803
Charting the Australian coast in the *Investigator*, becomes the first to circumnavigate the continent.

1803–1810
Is shipwrecked off the Great Barrier Reef and imprisoned as a spy on Île de France (Mauritius).

1810
Returns to England.

1814
A Voyage to Terra Australis is published; Flinders dies.

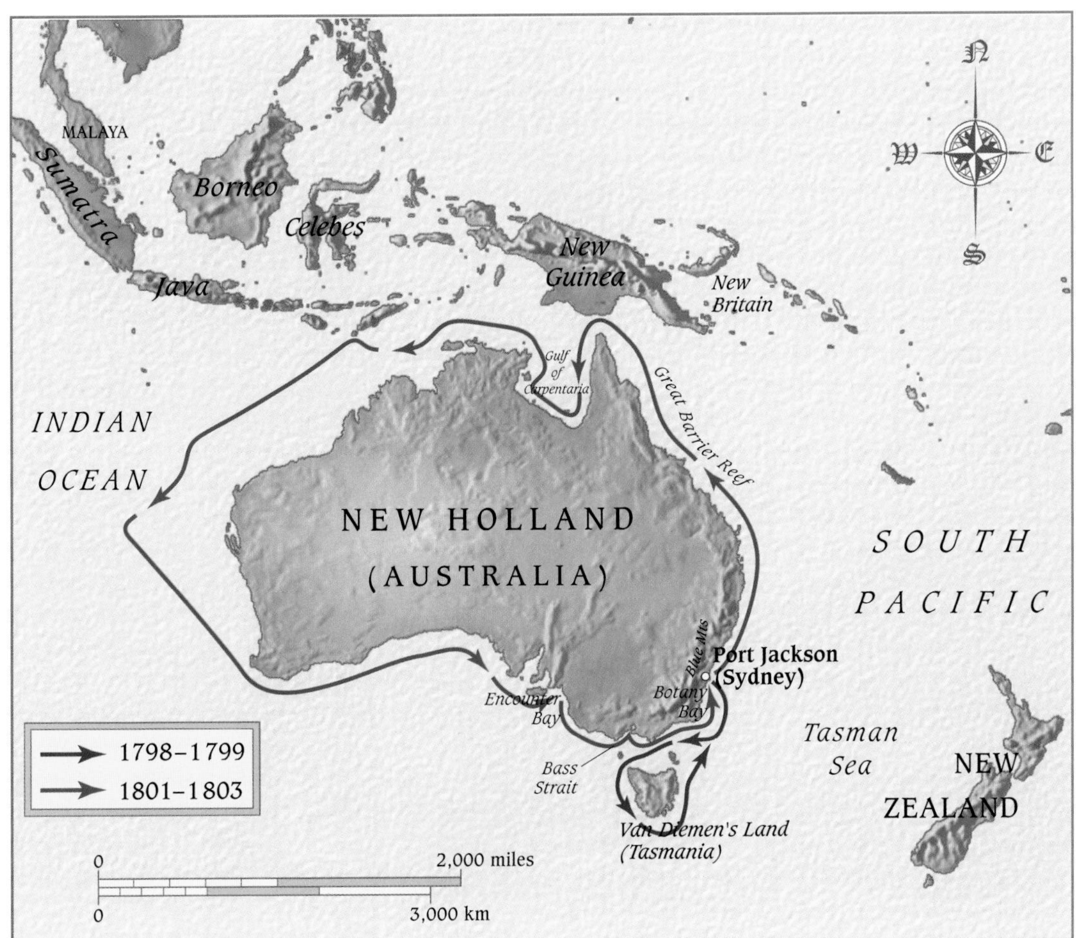

Left **This map shows the routes taken by Flinders in his voyages around Australia between 1798 and 1803.**

that point, promised to help. Flinders was appointed commander of HMS *Investigator*, which sailed from England in July 1801.

Circumnavigation of Australia

The circumnavigation of Australia began in December 1801. Flinders took an eastward (counterclockwise) route from the southwest. Meanwhile, the French explorer Nicolas Baudin (1754–1803) was also exploring the coastline as part of a mission to collect scientific specimens. The two men met in April 1802 at a place on the south coast, to the east of present-day Adelaide, later given the name Encounter Bay. Despite the political tension that existed between Britain and France, Flinders and Baudin put their differences aside, and the Englishman gave copies of his charts to his French rival.

By May 1802 Flinders had reached Port Jackson. From there he sailed north up the east coast of New Holland, along the Great Barrier Reef, until he rounded the Cape York Peninsula and entered the Gulf of Carpentaria on the northern coast. However, an outbreak of scurvy on the *Investigator*, together with the leaky condition of the ship, forced Flinders to abandon his survey. He returned to Port Jackson in June 1803 via a westerly route; with this achievment he became the first person to sail all the way around Australia.

Convicts as Colonists

In 1788 six shiploads of convicts (consisting of 564 men and 192 women) arrived in Botany Bay, Australia, from Britain. Their arrival marked the beginning of the colonization of Australia, just eighteen years after James Cook had claimed New South Wales (his name for eastern Australia) for Britain. From then until 1850, the British government sent around 162,000 convicts to Australia. They colonized the land and eventually became the founders of a nation.

Above **Nineteenth-century engravings, such as this one, informed Europeans about the lifestyle of the Australian aborigines, seen here hunting kangaroos with wooden spears.**

Shipwrecked and Imprisoned

Flinders was keen to complete his survey and planned to return to England to find a new ship for this purpose. On the voyage home he was shipwrecked off the Great Barrier Reef. He soon set sail again, but his ship was so rotten that, in December 1803, he was forced to put in at the French-held island of Île de France (present-day Mauritius). Flinders, unaware that Britain and France were at war, was imprisoned on the island for seven years.

On August 23, 1804, Flinders suggested in a letter to Sir Joseph Banks that New Holland be renamed:

I send you, Sir Joseph, a copy of my general chart of New Holland. . . . The propriety of the name Australia or Terra Australis, which I have applied to the whole of the body of what has generally been called New Holland, must be submitted to the approbation of the Admiralty and the learned in geography.

Matthew Flinders

Once back in England, Flinders wrote a book in which he described his exploration of the coastline of Australia. *A Voyage to Terra Australis* was published in 1814, but Flinders died the day after he received the first copy of his great work. In his book Flinders used the name Australia for the southern continent. He had long felt this name was more appropriate than New Holland, but his suggestion was not accepted by the British government until 1830.

Flinders's circumnavigation of Australia proved that the continent was a single landmass rather than a series of islands, as had been previously thought. His survey brought to an end a forty-year period of European exploration of the Pacific region that had begun with the voyages of James Cook.

SEE ALSO

• Cook, James • Great Britain

France

AT THE BEGINNING of the sixteenth century, Spain and Portugal were leading the global drive to discover and conquer new lands. King Francis I of France, determined that his country should emulate the Spanish and Portuguese pioneers, sent numerous French explorers to claim new lands. Most French explorers traveled to North America, but others ventured to Africa, Asia, and the Pacific.

The New World

In 1524 the Italian navigator Giovanni da Verrazzano was sent to explore the eastern coast of North America on behalf of Francis I. Verrazzano discovered the site of present-day New York harbor and traveled north to Newfoundland, where he visited the area that the local peoples referred to as Canada (a word that means "village" or "settlement").

However, in 1494 Pope Alexander VI had declared that only Spanish and Portuguese navigators could claim new colonies in the New World. French explorers risked excommunication from the Roman Catholic Church if they disobeyed this decree. In 1533 Francis I persuaded Pope Clement VII that the French should also be allowed to seek new territory in the Americas. The following year Francis I sent French explorers to North America to claim land for France, to search for riches, and to find the Northwest Passage—the legendary shortcut from the Atlantic to the Pacific Ocean that would provide a direct route from Europe to Asia.

Among these first explorers was Jacques Cartier (1491–1557), who traveled to present-day Canada and penetrated the Saint Lawrence River as far as the Lachine Rapids, a thousand miles (1,600 km) inland. French attempts to found a colony near present-day Quebec failed, but Cartier's explorations laid the basis for the fur trade with native people. He claimed Canada for his country, naming it New France.

Left **In 1534 Jacques Cartier landed at Gaspé Bay on the Canadian coast and took possession of that country in the name of France.**

The Rise of New France

Below **The struggle for Quebec was a decisive battle in the French and Indian War (1754–1763). This engraving shows the English war fleet arriving in Quebec in 1759.**

At the beginning of the seventeenth century, France increased its program of exploration. King Henry IV sent more colonists across the Atlantic and, in 1603, appointed a royal geographer and mapmaker. Among the new wave of explorers was Samuel de Champlain, whose task was to examine the waterways of New France and to choose sites for settlements. Having settled in Acadia (present-day Nova Scotia), in 1608 Champlain founded the city of Quebec on the site of a native settlement named Stadacona, which he intended to use as a base for the search for a route to China. Later, with local Indians as guides, he explored Ontario and Lake Huron. Farther south, in 1673 Louis Jolliet, a fur trader, and Jacques Marquette, a missionary, explored 2,500 miles (4,000 km) of the Mississippi River. Meanwhile, colonists were drawn to New France in numbers sufficient to ensure its survival.

1494
Treaty of Tordesillas divides the New World between Spain and Portugal.

1524
Giovanni da Verrazzano explores the east coast of North America.

1533
Pope Clement VII allows France to explore the New World.

1534
Jacques Cartier claims Canada for France.

1598–1603
Henry IV of France sends men and women to present-day Nova Scotia.

1608
Samuel de Champlain founds Quebec.

1615
Champlain explores Lake Huron.

1663
King Louis XIV makes New France a royal province.

1673
Jolliet and Marquette explore the Mississippi River.

1754–1763
The French and Indian War is fought.

Despite wars over territory and trading rights with the British and the native Iroquois, New France grew in size. By the mid-eighteenth century, the province extended from Hudson Bay in the north to Louisiana in the south and from the Mississippi valley in the west to the Saint Lawrence valley in the east.

The French and Indian War

Fought between France and Great Britain, the French and Indian War (1754–1763) led eventually to the end of New France. The two countries disagreed on whether the upper Ohio River valley was part of the British or the French empire. France lost the war, and in 1763 the Treaty of Paris gave all but the islands of Saint Pierre and Miquelon to the British. The inhabitants of New France became British subjects, and in 1791 the area reverted to its former name, Canada.

Above **The fur trade between the French colonists and native inhabitants of New France was worth a great deal of money.**

1763
The Treaty of Paris signals the end of New France.

1766–1769
Louis-Antoine de Bougainville circumnavigates the globe.

1791
The name Canada is officially restored.

1824–1828
René Caillié travels to Tombouctou (in West Africa) and across the Sahara Desert.

The Fur Trade

In the seventeenth century fur became very popular in Europe, yet it remained in short supply. After Jacques Cartier first traded with the Micmac tribe in 1534, it became clear that there was a plentiful supply of fur in New France, and French explorers realized that there was money to be made from trading in fur.

In exchange for fur, the colonists gave tools and other European goods to native Americans, who also supplied valuable knowledge about unexplored areas and tips for survival. The search for new supplies of fur went hand in hand with much French exploration in North America. However, the quest for profit led to frequent conflicts among the Indian tribes, the British, and the French. When Britain won New France in 1763, the British also took over the country's fur trade.

Above **French soldiers are depicted here raising their flag over the historic West African trading post of Timbuktu, which the French captured in 1893.**

Exploration around the World

Although French overseas territorial expansion was concentrated on North America, French explorers traveled to other parts of the world. From 1766 to 1769 Louis-Antoine de Bougainville sailed around the globe and claimed several islands and countries for France. Francis Garnier (1839–1873) explored the area surrounding the Mekong River in Vietnam. However, neither explorer added much territory to France's empire. In the 1820s René Caillié (1799–1838) became the first European explorer to visit and return safely from the West African city of Tombouctou (Timbuktu). The most influential French explorer of the twentieth century was Jacques Cousteau, whose unforgettable films revealed a previously hidden undersea world.

SEE ALSO

- Bougainville, Louis-Antoine de
- Cartier, Jacques
- Champlain, Samuel de
- Cousteau, Jacques-Yves
- Exploration and Geographical Societies
- Garnier, Francis
- Jolliet, Louis
- Verrazzano, Giovanni da

René Caillié recorded his first impressions of Timbuktu (present-day Tombouctou, Mali):

At length, we arrived safely at Timbuktu. . . . On entering this mysterious city, which is an object of curiosity and research to the civilized nations of Europe, I experienced an indescribable satisfaction . . . however . . . I looked around and found that the sight before me . . . did not answer my expectations. I had formed a totally different idea of the grandeur and wealth of Timbuktu. The city presented, at first view, nothing but a mass of ill-looking houses built of earth. Nothing was to be seen in all directions but immense plains of quicksand of a yellowish white color. The sky was a pale red as far as the horizon: all nature wore a dreary aspect, and the most profound silence prevailed; not even the warbling of a bird was to be heard. Still, though I cannot account for the impression, there was something imposing in the aspect of a great city, raised in the midst of sands, and the difficulties surmounted by its founders cannot fail to excite admiration.

René Caillié, *Travels through Central Africa to Timbuktu*

Franklin, John

THE ENGLISH EXPLORER Sir John Franklin (1786–1847) is remembered for his involvement in the worst disaster in the history of Arctic exploration. In 1845 he sailed with two ships in search of a northwest passage, a waterway through the North American Arctic that would connect the Atlantic and Pacific Oceans. Neither Franklin nor any of his 128 men were seen alive by Europeans again.

Born in Lincolnshire in eastern England, John Franklin joined the British navy at the age of fourteen. As a midshipman he took part in the Napoleonic wars (fought between Britain and France from 1793 to 1815) and later accompanied his uncle Matthew Flinders on the first voyage around Australia (1801–1803).

When the wars ended, the British navy needed a new role. Sir John Barrow, the naval secretary, decided that British ships should be dedicated to exploration, with the aim of filling in the many blank spaces that remained on maps of the world.

The Man Who Ate His Boots

On his first expedition, from 1819 to 1822, Franklin traveled overland from Hudson Bay to map the unexplored northern coast of Canada. The expedition was a disaster and ended in starvation, murder, and cannibalism. Forced to eat lichen scraped from rocks and even their own boiled shoes, ten of Franklin's twenty men starved to death. One man, Robert Hood, was murdered by Michel Teroahauté, a hunter who had secretly been feeding the others flesh from the corpses. When John Richardson became convinced that Teroahauté was guilty of cannibalism and the murder of Hood, he shot Teroahauté dead. In England Franklin's account of his sufferings made him famous. He became known as "the man who ate his boots."

Franklin's second expedition to the Arctic (1825–1827) was much more successful. He traced Canada's Mackenzie River to the sea and then mapped 610 miles (982 km) of unknown coastline. In 1829 he was honored for this achievement with a knighthood.

Below **In this illustration from Franklin's account of his 1825–1827 expedition, a group of Inuit, the native people of the Canadian Arctic, are startled to see the white explorers. Franklin wrote that they made furious gestures and shook their bows and arrows.**

To Find the Northwest Passage

By the 1840s the British navy had explored the eastern and western ends of a potential northwest passage in the Canadian Arctic. In 1845 Franklin was appointed to complete the charting of the passage. On May 19 he sailed from London in command of two large and well-equipped ships, the *Erebus* and the *Terror*.

In July, after completing his crossing of the Atlantic, Franklin met two whaling ships off the coast of Greenland. Captain Dannett, one of the whalers, welcomed Franklin and his officers on board his ship. Dannett wrote in his log, "Both ships' crews are all well and in remarkable spirits, expecting to finish the operation in good time." This contact was the last that any white person had with Franklin and his men.

Below **Sir John Franklin, Arctic explorer, depicted in a lithograph by Thomas Maguire (1821–1895).**

The Search for Franklin

In 1848 the first of many search expeditions began to comb the Arctic for signs of Franklin. Although he was never found, the search party succeeded in mapping the entire Northwest Passage and adjacent islands. In August 1850 on Beechey Island, Captain Erasmus Ommanney found the camp where Franklin had spent his first winter in the Arctic. Later the same month Captain William Penny discovered the graves of three sailors whose wooden headstones recorded that they had died in January and April 1846.

Inuit Story

In 1854 the explorer Dr. John Rae met some Inuit (a native people of the Arctic), who told him a chilling story. They said that four years before, they had met a group of forty hungry white men dragging a small boat over the ice in the direction of the Back River. Using signs, the strangers indicated that their ship had been crushed by the ice.

Later that same year the Inuit found the bodies of most of these men west of the Back

1819–1822
John Franklin leads his first expedition to the Canadian Arctic.

1825–1827
Leads his second expedition to the Canadian Arctic.

May 19, 1845
Departs London.

July 28, 1845
The *Erebus* and *Terror* are last seen, by whalers, in Melville Bay off Greenland.

August 1845
Franklin enters Lancaster Sound, Wellington Channel, and sails north around Cornwallis Island.

Winter 1845–Spring 1846
Camps on Beechey Island.

Summer 1846
Sails from Beechey Island south down Peel Sound and through Franklin Strait.

September 12, 1846
Franklin's ships become trapped in the ice north of King William Island.

June 11, 1847
Franklin dies.

April 22, 1848
Led by Captain Francis Crozier, the men abandon the ships and set off south.

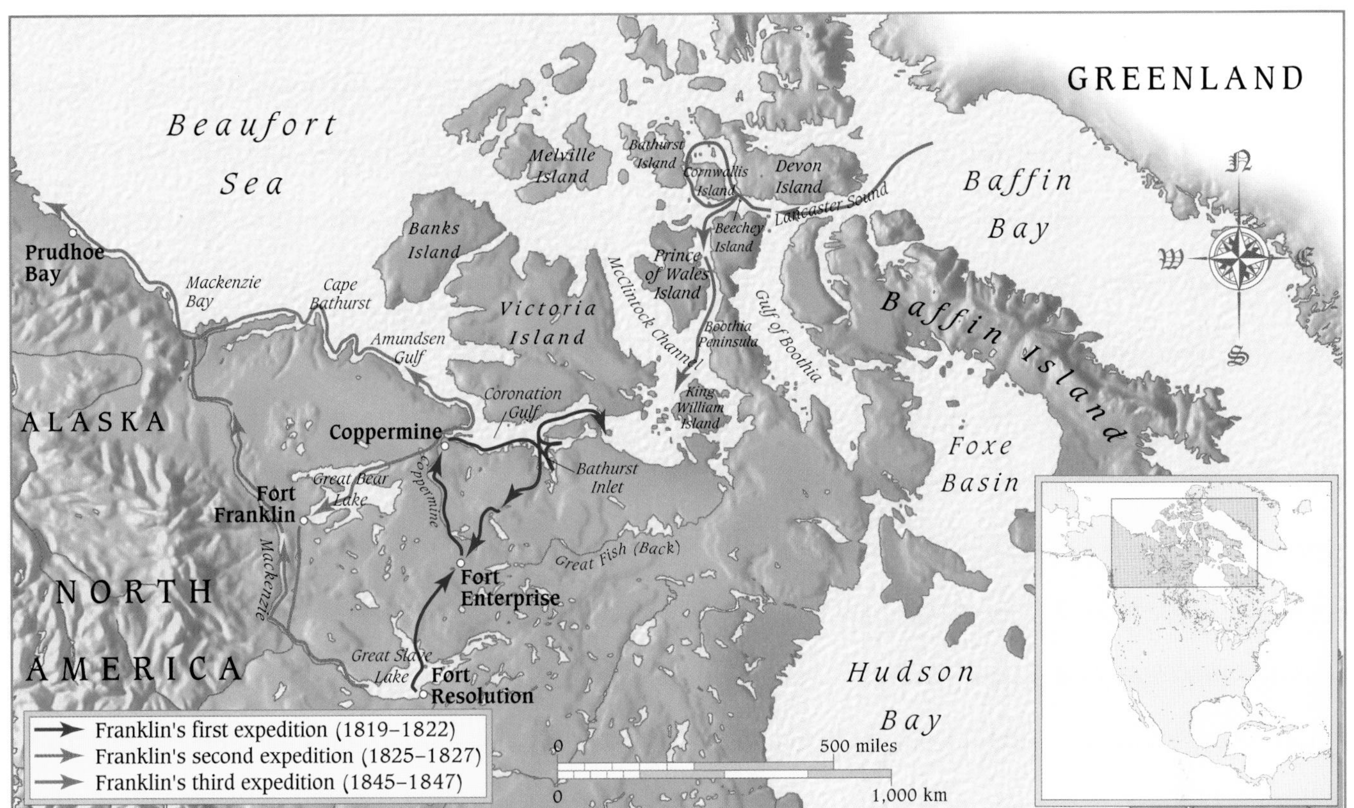

Above **John Franklin's expeditions to the Canadian Arctic.**

River. Bones with knife marks on them showed that the dead had been butchered and eaten by their companions. The Inuit sold Rae objects they had collected, including a gold watch and spoons bearing the initials of Franklin's officers.

Discovery of a Note

In 1859 Captain Francis McClintock searched Prince of Wales Island, where he found more relics and skeletons. At Victory Point on King William Island, McClintock also discovered a note left by Franklin's officers that recorded their route from Beechey Island to the sea off King William Island, where, on September 12, 1846, their ships had become icebound. According to the note, "Sir John Franklin died on the 11th June 1847; and the total loss by deaths in this expedition has been, to this date, nine officers and fifteen men." After Franklin's death, Captain Crozier had taken command. In April 1848, after nineteen months trapped in the ice, Crozier had decided to abandon the ships and to head south with 105 remaining men. However, the note presented as many problems as it solved. Why had so many men died? What had gone wrong?

1848
First search expeditions reach the Canadian Arctic.

August 27, 1850
Three graves are discovered on Beechey Island.

1854
Dr. John Rae hears the Inuit stories of starving white men.

May 5, 1859
Francis McClintock finds a note recording the abandonment of the ships.

Franklin's Ships

The *Erebus* and the *Terror* were the best-equipped ships ever sent on a voyage of exploration. The most advanced scientific equipment was on board, including a camera, only recently invented. Each ship had its own library, totaling 2,900 books. Among the supplies, enough for over three years, were eight thousand tins of meat, soup, and vegetables.

Above **This relief, in which the sculptor has imagined Franklin's funeral, is part of a monument to the explorer in Waterloo Place, London.**

Furthermore, the note gave no indication of why Crozier abandoned the ships in the spring, before the arrival of the warm weather that might have freed the ships. Why did he head south toward territory where Franklin had almost starved to death on his first expedition? How could the note, describing an 1848 abandonment by over a hundred men, be reconciled with the Inuit tale of a meeting with forty white men in 1850?

A modern Franklin investigator, David C. Woodman, has looked at other Inuit stories to find the answers. Woodman believes that Crozier, faced by an outbreak of scurvy, was heading south not to escape but to hunt for fresh meat. According to Inuit stories the ships were not finally abandoned in 1848 but were remanned for a time after that.

The Franklin mystery remains unsolved. Expeditions continue to search the Arctic for more clues to explain what happened and in the hope that, one day, the wrecks of the *Erebus* and the *Terror* will be found, along with John Franklin's body, preserved in the ice.

Lead Poisoning

In 1984 and 1986 Dr. Owen Beattie dug up the bodies of the three sailors buried on Beechey Island and found them perfectly preserved. Tests showed that they had suffered from lead poisoning. By itself the amount of lead was not fatal, yet it would have further weakened the men, who were already ill from scurvy and possibly botulism. The source of this lead was found lying around Beechey Island: empty food tins. Franklin's tins had been crudely sealed with lead, and the food had been contaminated.

SEE ALSO

• Flinders, Matthew • Northwest Passage

FRÉMONT, JOHN

WITH THE PUBLICATION of his reports on expeditions in the American West, John Charles Frémont, born in 1813 in Georgia, became one of the most famous American explorers. Frémont's marriage to Jessie Benton was extremely advantageous: his father-in-law was a powerful politician who gained Frémont his important commissions, and his wife was a skilled writer who helped to turn him into a hero. Frémont's work made an important contribution to the promotion of America's expansion westward. He died in New York in 1890.

EARLY LIFE

After John Frémont's father, Charles Fremon, died in 1818, the family moved to Charleston, South Carolina, where a lawyer befriended them and saw to John's education at the College of Charleston. Despite excelling in Greek, Latin, and mathematics, John was expelled for poor attendance. From 1833 to 1835, he taught mathematics and navigation to young officers aboard a ship that sailed to South America. In 1836 he joined a party surveying a railroad route between Charleston and Cincinnati, Ohio. Frémont enjoyed the experience, and the following year he won a commission as a second lieutenant in the U.S. Army Corps of Topographical Engineers.

HEADING WEST

On Frémont's first two expeditions, to the area north of the Mississippi and Missouri Rivers, he learned much about topography, cartography, and life in the American wilderness. Back in Washington he worked closely with the expedition's leader to finalize the maps they had prepared. During this time he met Senator Thomas Hart Benton of Missouri, who firmly believed that the United States should expand to the west. Frémont and Benton's sixteen-year-old daughter, Jessie, fell in love and married. Though he had opposed the marriage, Benton decided to use his new son-in-law to advance his expansionist goals.

Below **John Charles Frémont added the *t* and the accent to his father's last name, perhaps to give himself an air of romance.**

Above **After Frémont completed the report of his second expedition, Congress ordered the two reports published together and had ten thousand copies printed. Publication took place just after the opening of the Oregon Trail and helped spur thousands of Americans to move west in covered wagons.**

The Pathfinder

From 1842 to 1846, Frémont carried out three major explorations of the West. In each case Senator Benton gained him the commission. The reports of his exploits, which were written with the assistance of Jessie, presented Frémont as "the pathfinder," a daring explorer who blazed new trails. In truth, the trails were not new; Frémont relied on Kit Carson and other experienced frontiersmen to guide him. Nevertheless, Frémont's enthusiastic praise for the fertile lands on the Pacific coast helped persuade many Americans to move west—and his maps helped lead them there. Frémont was also the first to explain the nature of the Great Basin, the harsh highlands between the Rocky Mountains and the Sierra Nevadas.

The first expedition simply followed the Oregon Trail halfway. After going through the south pass, Frémont headed north to explore the Wind River Mountains. He and several of his company climbed a 13,500-foot (4,115 m) mountain, which Frémont thought was the highest point in the Rockies. After returning to Saint Louis, Frémont and Jessie dashed off a stirring report to Congress.

Congress approved a new journey aimed at reaching the Pacific coast. Frémont left in 1843 and rode all the way to the Columbia River, which marks the border between the present-day states of Washington and Oregon. With fresh supplies Frémont decided to take a circuitous route home. Leading his men south and skirting the eastern edge of the Sierra Nevada range, Frémont was determined to cross the mountains, despite the danger of doing so in winter. After much hardship he finally led his men to safety. In the spring of 1844, the party began a long return trip. The men left California from the south, crossed the southern edge of the Great Basin, and after more than a year, arrived back in Saint Louis.

Once again Frémont and Jessie produced an inspiring and informative report. It praised California and Oregon, revealed the weak Mexican hold on California, and proved that a long-imagined river that ran from the Rockies west to the Pacific was a myth. The maps that resulted from this expedition were of great use to later travelers.

Below **Jessie Frémont helped her husband in many ways. When, in 1843, she received a letter warning her husband not to begin his second expedition, she ignored it and told him to leave at once.**

Jessie Benton Frémont *1824–1902*

Jessie Benton's father was a successful politician, and her mother came from an established Virginia family. Educated largely by her father, she inherited both his able mind and strong will. When she met the charismatic Frémont, she ignored her parents' objections and secretly married him. After a reconciliation father, daughter, and son-in-law worked closely together. While Frémont explored, Jessie lived with her parents and acted as her father's hostess. When the explorer returned, she collaborated on his reports. The couple suffered some personal tragedies, including the death of two infant children and the destruction of their San Francisco home in a fire. When they lost their fortune after the Civil War, Jessie wrote books to support them. She outlived her husband by twelve years.

1813
John Frémont is born in Savannah, Georgia.

1829–1831
Attends the College of Charleston but is dismissed before graduation.

1836–1837
Works on a railroad survey.

1838
Joins U.S. Army Corps of Topographical Engineers.

1841
Elopes with Jessie Benton.

1842
Leads first western expedition.

1843–1844
Leads second western expedition.

1845–1846
Leads third western expedition, at the end of which he participates in the conquest of California.

1848
Leads fourth western expedition.

1856
Loses presidential election.

1861
Serves briefly and poorly in Union army during the Civil War.

1890
Dies.

War with Mexico

Frémont's third expedition helped to bring California into the United States. In 1845 he was sent to explore the Pacific coast region, although the area was still part of Mexico. Later in the same year, war broke out between the United States and Mexico. Supported by Frémont, American settlers in California revolted against Mexican authority there and declared an independent republic. Frémont and his party arrived in 1846, and soon afterward they took part in battles that helped the American military win control over California.

By this time Frémont was not only the Pathfinder but also an important factor in helping the United States expand to the Pacific. However, Frémont's involvement with the U.S. Army ended badly. A personal conflict with the army officer in charge of the American forces in California resulted in Frémont being court-martialed. He was

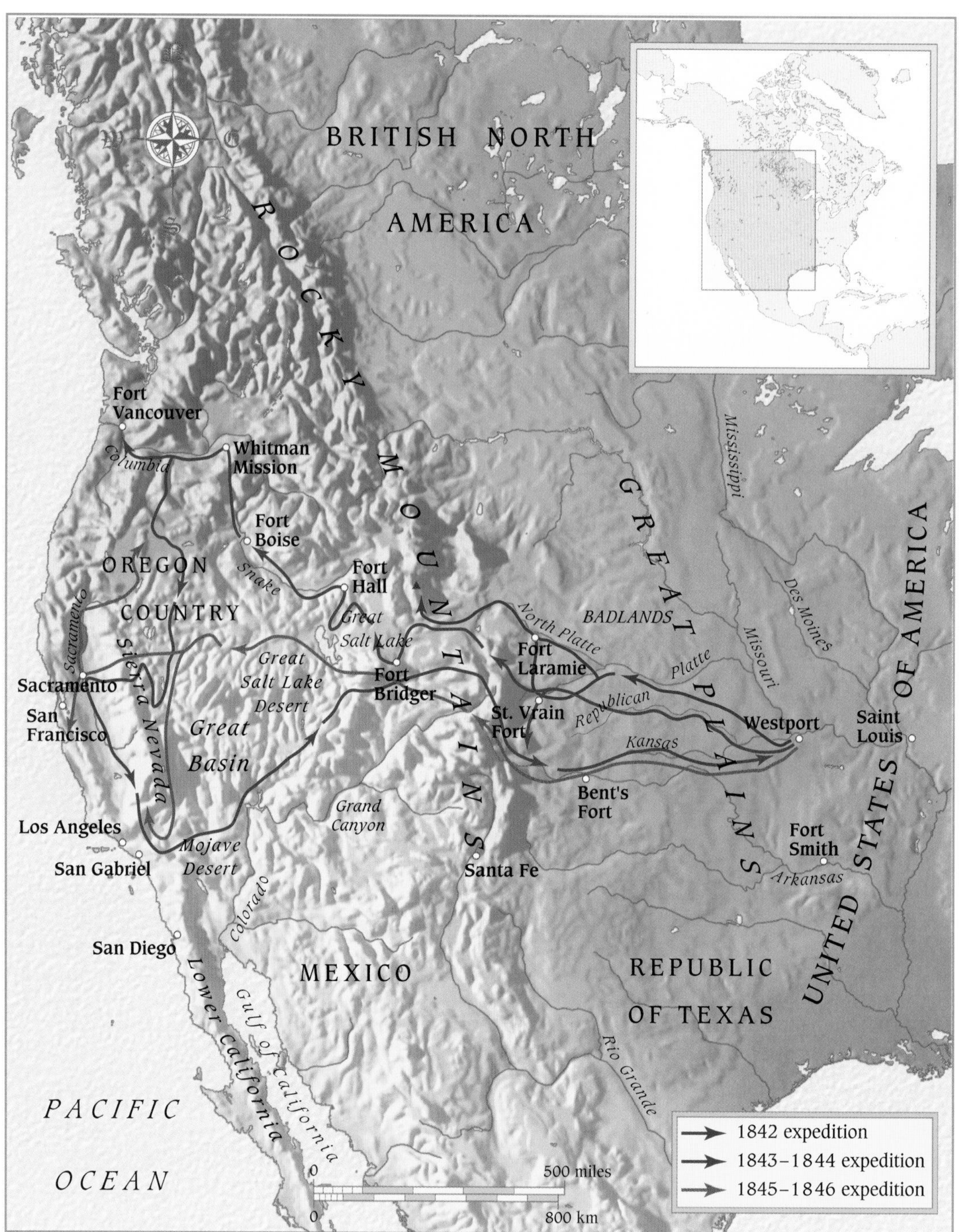

Right **This map details Frémont's government-sponsored expeditions in the American West, between 1842 and 1846.**

Jessie Frémont helped her husband add a dash of romance to his expedition reports:

I sprang upon the summit, and another step would have [plunged] me into an immense snow field five hundred feet below. To the edge of this field was a sheer icy precipice; and then, with a gradual fall, the field sloped off for about a mile, until it struck the foot of another lower ridge. I stood on a narrow crest, about three feet in width. . . . As soon as I had gratified the first feelings of curiosity, I descended, and each man ascended in his turn; for I would only allow one at a time to mount the unstable and precarious slab, which it seemed a breath would hurl into the abyss below. We mounted the barometer in the snow of the summit, and fixing a ramrod in a crevice, unfurled the national flag to wave in the breeze where never flag waved before.

John Frémont, *Memoirs*

Above **The Republicans ran the Pathfinder for president in 1856 under the slogan Free Soil, Free Speech, Free Men, Frémont.**

found guilty of insubordination and saved only when President James Polk suspended his sentence. Angered by his treatment, Frémont resigned his commission.

Politician, General, and Faded Star

In 1848 Frémont led a privately funded expedition that attempted to plot a good route for a railroad to the Pacific. Once again he tried a dangerous midwinter crossing of the massive and treacherous San Juan mountain range in southern Colorado. This time, however, eleven of his men died in the attempt.

Despite this disaster, it seemed that Frémont's luck had turned. Gold had been discovered at several places in California, including land that had been purchased for Frémont. Suddenly, he and Jessie were very rich. When California became a state in 1850, he was elected to a brief term in the U.S. Senate. His service was undistinguished, and he spent much of the next two years in Europe. However, in the growing debate over the spread of slavery to the territories, Frémont took a firm antislavery line. As a result the newly formed Republican Party nominated him for president in 1856. After losing the election, Frémont returned to California. When the Civil War broke out in 1861, Frémont won appointment as a general, but after botching two different assignments, he resigned.

After the war Frémont's star faded. He lost his land in California and lost the remainder of his fortune in a failed railroad business. He and Jessie settled in California, where he lived for the remainder of his life.

SEE ALSO
- Bridger, Jim
- Carson, Kit

FROBISHER, MARTIN

Below **Elizabethan explorer Martin Frobisher was also a ruthless privateer.**

THE ENGLISH SEA CAPTAIN Sir Martin Frobisher (c. 1535–1594) made his first voyages to the slave markets of West Africa. In the 1570s he made three voyages to the Canadian Arctic; the aim of the first was to find a northwest passage that could be used as a direct sea route from Europe to the riches of Asia, and the second two were mining ventures to recover gold that turned out to be nonexistent. Frobisher, a privateer as well as an explorer, played a key role in defeating the Spanish armada in 1588 and was mortally wounded in battle against the Spanish in 1594.

Martin Frobisher's first sea voyages, as an apprenticed cabin boy at fourteen, took him to the slave ports along the coast of West Africa. In 1562 he was arrested by the Portuguese on charges of piracy and imprisoned at the fortress of Mina (in present-day Ghana). Frobisher avoided trial, however, and by 1565 was commanding his own ship and engaging in raids on Spanish merchantmen.

SEARCH FOR THE NORTHWEST PASSAGE

In the sixteenth century many navigation experts believed that the Atlantic and Pacific Oceans were connected by a northwest passage that led through the waters of the Canadian Arctic. Merchants in London were

c. 1535
Martin Frobisher is born in Yorkshire, northern England.

1549
Voyages to Africa at the age of fourteen.

1565
Is appointed captain of his own ship.

1576
Makes first voyage to North America.

1577
Makes second voyage to North America.

1578
Makes third voyage to North America.

desperate to find this sea passage, as it would give England its own trade route to the Indies, one that would bypass the powerful Spanish Empire far to the south. Thanks to his patron Ambrose Dudley, the earl of Warwick, Frobisher found the backers to fund an expedition to the North American Arctic.

Frobisher and thirty-five men set sail from Deptford in June 1576 in two small ships, the *Gabriel* and the *Michael*, each weighing twenty-eight tons (25,400 kg) , and a pinnace of eleven tons (10,000 kg). After rounding the Shetlands and skirting Greenland, the ships ran into a storm. The pinnace was lost, and the *Michael* returned to England. The *Gabriel* reached the Canadian coast in late July and entered a water channel that Frobisher thought was a strait but was later revealed to be a bay. After claiming the surrounding land for Queen Elizabeth, late in the summer, with five men lost in an encounter with Inuit and conditions becoming increasingly icy, Frobisher set sail for England. On the way he came across an Inuit fisherman in his kayak and took him back to England. The strange native and his unusual boat caused a sensation in Elizabethan London, but with no resistance to European germs, he soon died.

Before leaving for home, Frobisher collected samples of a heavy dark stone that glittered when it was heated. He hoped that he had found a source of precious metal to rival the gold and silver mines controlled by the Spanish in their American colonies.

1585
Sails to the Spanish West Indies with Sir Francis Drake.

1588
Is knighted for his part in defeating the Spanish armada.

1592
Joins Sir Walter Raleigh's voyage to harry Spanish fleets.

1594
Is wounded in France and dies at Plymouth.

Testing the Ores

In the sixteenth century, as the ores of precious metals came to Europe from all over the world, the work of a group of skilled men called assayers became important. It was the assayer's job to test these ores, measure their weight, and judge their likely value. The royal assayer at the English court dismissed Frobisher's "black earth" as merely iron pyrites, or fool's gold. However, after a second assayer concluded that Frobisher's rocks did contain some low-grade gold, a number of London merchants were encouraged to give Frobisher the money for a second expedition to the Arctic.

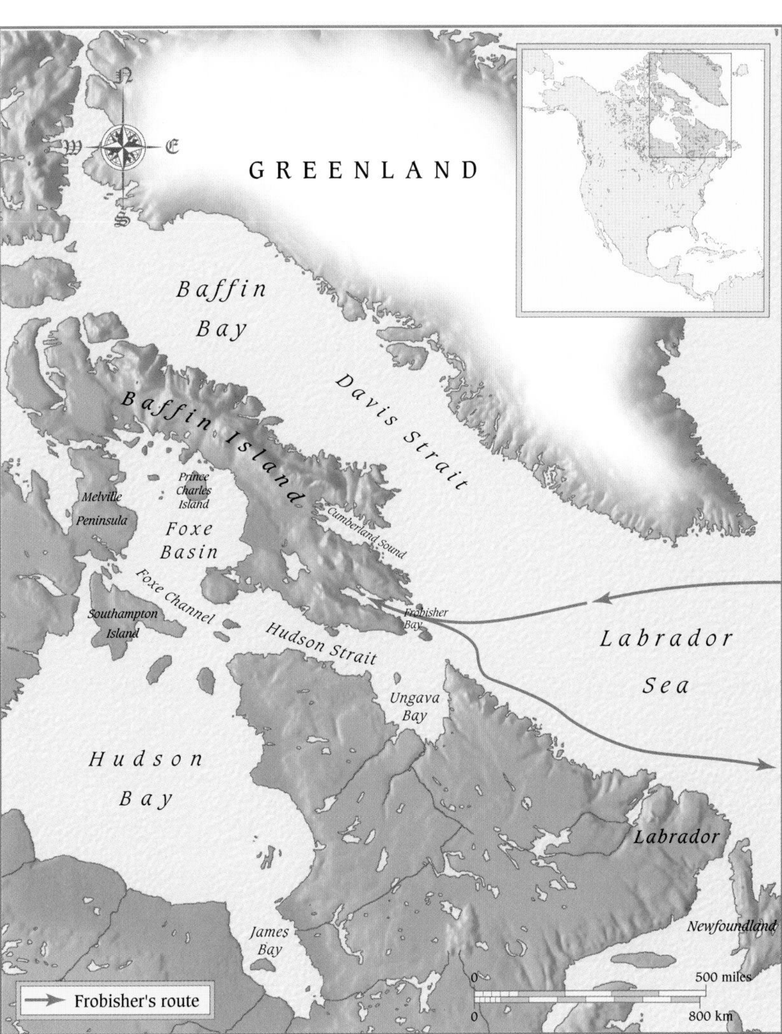

Above **Frobisher's 1576 voyage in search of the Northwest Passage.**

Below **On Frobisher's second voyage , the Inuit used bows and arrows to defend themselves against Frobisher's matchlock guns. After these initial conflicts, the Inuit avoided further contact with the Europeans.**

Further Voyages to North America

As a result of his find, Frobisher was employed by the newly founded Cathay Company of London merchants. They ordered him to find more of the black ore and to send one of his three ships to look for the Northwest Passage. Frobisher left Harwich (in eastern England) in 1577 and spent the summer months mining over two hundred tons of minerals and engaging in renewed conflict with the Inuit. When Frobisher returned to England, his holds were full of ore, but he had made no further search for a passage to the Pacific.

On his third voyage to the Arctic (1578), Frobisher commanded a fleet of fifteen vessels and over four hundred men. In the Arctic waste of Baffin Island, he planned to establish a settlement of one hundred men who would continue the job of mining for

precious metals. However—perhaps fortunately for the potential "winterers"—the ship carrying most of the wood and tools needed for the construction of the settlement sank in bad weather. Frobisher managed to build a single small stone house on an island that he named after the countess of Warwick (present-day Kodlurnan Island). After collecting over two thousand tons of black rock, Frobisher sailed home. His hopes of wealth vanished when the rocks were proved to be worthless. In fact, Frobisher lost much of his own money when the Cathay Company investors took him to the law courts, having accused Frobisher of deceiving them.

Frobisher's voyages gave strong indications of the existence of a northwest passage, a notion that further English exploration, especially the voyages of Luke Foxe (1631) and Thomas James (1631–1632) temporarily laid to rest. Frobisher also showed that the north part of North America was too barren to support the establishment of colonies. After Frobisher, English adventurers looked farther south when planning new settlements in the Americas.

Frobisher and the Inuit

Frobisher and his crew were the first Europeans encountered by the Inuit, the native peoples of the Canadian Arctic, since Norse voyages to Inuit lands six hundred years earlier. Initially the relationship between the English and the Inuit was good, and Frobisher was able to use sign language to trade for fresh meat. However, there was soon trouble between them. Five of Frobisher's crew disobeyed orders by visiting the Inuit encampment. When they did not return, Frobisher took an Inuit hostage. The man and his kayak were taken to England, where they caused a sensation at the royal court. Unfortunately, the hostage soon died, probably as a result of the unfamiliar germs he came into contact with. The following year Frobisher returned to the Arctic and found the bloodied clothing of his five missing crewmen. A fight broke out, and an Inuit man, woman, and child were captured. All three died within a month after reaching England. The Inuit avoided further contact with Frobisher and his men.

Fighting the Spanish

The Cathay Company was bankrupted by Frobisher's failed northern voyages. However, Frobisher managed to secure his own fortune by serving as vice admiral in Sir Francis Drake's fleet. Frobisher played an important part in the success of Drake's raids on the Spanish bases in the West Indies in 1585. He won an enormous amount of booty and became wealthy as a result.

Frobisher was knighted in 1588 for his part in the defeat of the Spanish armada. He bought an estate in Yorkshire, in northern England, but soon grew tired of country life. In 1592 Frobisher set sail again, this time in the company of Sir Walter Raleigh. The purpose of Raleigh's expedition was to attack the Spanish treasure fleets that were transporting large quantities of gold from Panama to Europe. Frobisher was mortally wounded in 1594 near Brest, in Brittany, northern France, while trying to relieve Fort Crozon, which was under siege by the Spanish.

Although Martin Frobisher left no maps of his voyages into the Arctic, his attempt to locate a northwest passage to Asia served as an inspiration for a great many sailors in the centuries that followed.

SEE ALSO

- Drake, Francis • Northwest Passage
- Raleigh, Walter

Gagarin, Yury

YURY ALEKSEYEVICH GAGARIN WAS born on March 9, 1934, in Klushino in Russia, then part of the Soviet Union. In 1961 he became the first person to travel into space and to orbit the earth. He died in 1968.

Early Years

Yury Gagarin grew up on a collective (state-owned) farm about a hundred miles west of Moscow. His parents contributed toward the running of the farm—his father worked as a carpenter and bricklayer, and his mother as a milkmaid.

Below **Yury Gagarin, the first person in space.**

After World War II Gagarin went to a technical school near Moscow to learn metalwork. However, his real ambition was to fly, and in his spare time he took lessons at a local flying school. Gagarin proved to be a very able pilot (he first flew solo in 1955), and as soon as he graduated from technical school, he entered the Soviet air force. Although he quickly became a test pilot—a dangerous job that involves flying newly designed aircraft—Gagarin's ambitions were not yet satisfied.

The First Person in Space

In the 1950s, with the program still in its infancy, the directors of the Soviet space program were planning the first manned trip into space. Potential cosmonauts (the Russian name for astronauts) were selected from among the state's best test pilots. Gagarin decided that he wanted to be chosen to fly into space, and in 1959 he volunteered to become a cosmonaut.

Gagarin impressed the instructors with his flying skills and was given top marks. Then, on April 9, 1961, Gagarin was selected to make the historic first space journey. Just three days later he climbed aboard the Soviet spacecraft *Vostok 1*. At 9:07 AM local time, Gagarin was propelled out of the earth's atmosphere and into space by a powerful rocket. The first words that he spoke were, "I see earth. It's so beautiful."

Right **In 1965 *Vostok 1*, the spacecraft in which Gagarin had made his historic journey to space, was first shown to the public.**

Vostok 1

Gagarin's spacecraft was made up of two modules that weighed a total of 4.75 tons (4,300 kg). He traveled in a spherical module with three tiny portholes. As Soviet scientists did not know how weightlessness would affect their cosmonaut, *Vostok 1* was controlled by radio signals sent from a computer on earth. However, a key, sealed in an envelope, was sent with Gagarin. In an emergency he could use this key to override the spacecraft's controls. Also on board was enough food and water for ten days, in case the equipment failed to send the spacecraft straight back to earth. Scientists had calculated that it would take the spacecraft ten days to return to earth naturally.

The second module held the engine, as well as life-support and communications equipment, part of whose purpose was to relay information on the condition of the pilot back to earth. The two modules that made up *Vostok 1* were mounted on a rocket that measured 125.85 feet (38.36 m) in length and was designed to fire in three stages.

The final piece of equipment on board *Vostok 1* was the most secret—the ejector seat. After reentering earth's atmosphere, Gagarin ejected from the spacecraft at a height of 22,965 feet (7,000 m) and parachuted safely back down to earth. However, at that time the rules laid down by the World Air Sports Federation (a body established to promote air and space flight) stated that in order to qualify for a world record, a pilot had to return to earth with his spacecraft. The Soviet Union later admitted the truth, but Gagarin is still recognized as the first person to make a successful space flight.

Back Down to Earth

Traveling at a height of 203 miles (327 km) above the earth, *Vostok 1* took 1 hour and 48 minutes to complete its orbit and returned to earth at 10:55 AM.

As the first person in space, Gagarin became an instant celebrity. After his historic flight the Soviet Union honored him with awards, named streets after him, and sent him on publicity tours around the world. Gagarin later took on the responsibility of training other cosmonauts before becoming a test pilot once more. Tragically, he was killed in a plane crash in March 1968, when he was only thirty-four years old. The ashes of the first space traveler were laid to rest inside the Kremlin wall.

After landing on earth Yury Gagarin made the following official statement:

. . . there was a good view of the earth, which had a very distinct and pretty blue halo. It had a smooth transition from pale blue, blue, dark blue, violet and absolutely black. It was a magnificent picture.

Left **This Russian postcard celebrates Gagarin's pioneering orbit of earth. It was one of many honors he received in his short life.**

SEE ALSO
- Russia
- Spacecraft
- Space Exploration

March 9, 1934
Yury Gagarin is born.

1951–1955
While a student at technical college, takes flying lessons in his spare time.

1955
Joins the Soviet air force cadet school; makes his first solo flight.

1957
Graduates from cadet school.

1959
Begins training as a cosmonaut.

April 9, 1961
Is told that he has been chosen to be the first person to journey into space.

April 12, 1961
Vostok 1, Gagarin's spacecraft, is launched into space and orbits the earth.

March 27, 1968
Gagarin is killed in a plane crash.

GAMA, VASCO DA

THE PORTUGUESE NAVIGATOR Vasco da Gama (c.1469–1525) was the first explorer to sail from Europe to India by way of the Cape of Good Hope, at the southern tip of Africa. His historic voyage, made between 1497 and 1499, opened a new trade route that would soon bring the spices of India directly to Europe by sea and vastly enlarge Portugal's role in world affairs.

"Bold in Any Undertaking"

Vasco da Gama was born into a noble family in Sines, a seaport in southern Portugal. Little historical information about his early life exists, but it is known that by the 1490s he had become a soldier and naval commander.

In 1497 King Manuel I, nicknamed "the Fortunate," decided to send an expedition to India. The Portuguese explorer Bartolomeu Dias had rounded Africa's southern tip in 1488, and so Manuel knew that it was possible to sail to India by this route. Dias helped to plan the new expedition, but the king chose da Gama to lead it, probably because of da Gama's forceful and decisive personality. The sixteenth-century historian João de Barros described da Gama as "bold in any undertaking, sharp in command, painstaking and quick to punish wrongdoers in the name of justice."

Below **The subject of this portrait, painted in Portugal in the 1520s, is thought to be Vasco da Gama.**

Voyage to India

Vasco da Gama sailed from Portugal on July 8, 1497, as captain of the *São Gabriel*, while his brother Paulo captained the *São Rafael*. The fleet also included a caravel called the *Berrio* and a supply ship. For the first part of the journey, Bartolomeu Dias accompanied the fleet on his caravel, the *São Cristovão*.

After stopping at the Cape Verde Islands to take on supplies and repair damage, the fleet sailed southwest and then east. The sailors saw no land for three months, longer than on any previous voyage. Eventually, on November 4, 1497, they saw the coast of South Africa.

Da Gama rounded the Cape of Good Hope and sailed into the Indian Ocean. In February 1498 there was an outbreak of scurvy, a disease caused by the lack of fresh food. According to an eyewitness account, "Many of our men fell ill here, their feet and hands swelling, and their gums growing over their teeth so that they could not eat."

Da Gama sailed up the East African coast and visited ports at Mozambique, Mombasa, and Malindi. As Muslims the local people did not welcome the arrival of Christians in their waters. It was with great difficulty that da Gama found a pilot to guide his fleet to India.

Arrival

The crossing was made in April 1498 and took just twenty-three days. In May da Gama reached Calicut, the most important trading center on the Indian coast. The first man sent ashore was a convict who had been brought to perform any dangerous tasks. He met two Muslims from North Africa who knew how to speak Spanish and greeted him with the famous words, "The Devil take you! What brought you here?"

Da Gama met the ruler of Calicut, called the samorin, who was unimpressed by the gifts the Portuguese offered him. The local

Right **Da Gama's route from Portugal on his first voyage around the Cape of Good Hope to India (1497–1498).**

Da Gama's Ships

The main vessel used by Portuguese explorers in the fifteenth century was called a caravel. Caravels were small light ships, usually rigged with lateen (triangular) sails, which are ideally suited for sailing into the wind and maneuvering in coastal waters. In 1488 Bartolomeu Dias had used caravels to sail around the Cape of Good Hope.

For da Gama's voyage Dias supervised the building of two ships, the *São Rafael* and the *São Gabriel*, which were bigger and stronger than caravels. It was hoped that these ships would be better able to withstand the stormy weather that had caused problems for Dias off the Cape of Good Hope.

Da Gama's ships were rigged not with lateen sails but with square sails, which work much better in front of a following wind. Unlike Dias, da Gama took advantage of the South Atlantic wind system, which blows in a huge counterclockwise circle. Dias had sailed down the coast of Africa, a route that often meant sailing into the wind. To avoid this problem, da Gama swung out into the South Atlantic so that the wind would always be behind him.

Muslim merchants also refused to trade with da Gama, so he was able to obtain only a few samples of spices to take back.

Return to Portugal

The voyage home was a disaster, for da Gama sailed at the time of year when the monsoon winds changed direction with the seasons. It took almost three months to cross the Indian Ocean, and thirty men died from scurvy. Da Gama finally reached Portugal in September 1499, with just 55 survivors from his original crew of 170.

Da Gama advised the king to send a large well-armed fleet to India to force the Indians to trade. He was too exhausted to command this expedition himself, so Pedro Álvares Cabral was chosen instead. Cabral built a trading post in Calicut, but the men he left ashore there were killed by Indians.

Below **This sixteenth-century tapestry celebrates da Gama's arrival in the port of Calicut.**

July 8, 1497
Vasco da Gama sets sail for India.

November 7, 1497
Da Gama's fleet reaches the west coast of South Africa.

November 22, 1497
Rounds the Cape of Good Hope.

March 2, 1498
Reaches Mozambique.

April 27, 1498
Sails from Malindi for India.

May 20, 1498
Reaches Calicut in India.

August 29, 1498
Leaves Calicut.

September 9, 1499
Returns to Portugal.

May 9, 1500
Pedro Álvares Cabral sails to India with a large fleet.

February 12, 1502
Da Gama sails with a new fleet to India.

October 30, 1503
Arrives in Calicut on second voyage.

October 1503
Returns to Portugal.

April 1524
Sets sail for India, with a fleet of fourteen ships.

December 24, 1524
Dies in Cochin, India.

Above **In April 1498 da Gama set up this stone cross at Malindi, in present-day Kenya, to claim the land for Portugal and for Christianity.**

The Portuguese mistakenly believed that the Hindus of India were Christians, because unlike Muslims or Jews, they used images for religious worship. In fact, these were images of Hindu gods. An eyewitness described a Hindu temple, which he believed to be a church:

In this church [da Gama] said his prayers and we with him. . . . Saints were painted on the walls of the church, wearing crowns. They were painted variously, with teeth protruding an inch from the mouth, and four or five arms.

Journal of the First Voyage of Vasco da Gama

Later Voyages

With powerful fleets Da Gama made two later voyages to India that helped to found a Portuguese overseas empire. On the first of these voyages, in 1502, he acted with a brutality that shocked even his own men. In October 1502 da Gama captured a ship carrying around three hundred Muslim pilgrims home to Calicut from the holy city of Mecca. According to a Portuguese eyewitness, Tomé Lopes, da Gama "had the said ship burnt with those who were on it, very cruelly and without pity."

Da Gama's brutality was a deliberate revenge for the deaths of the Portuguese in Calicut. He wrote to the samorin of Calicut that he had killed the pilgrims to demonstrate how the Portuguese acted when anybody wronged them. In truth, his intention was to spread terror along the Indian coast so that local rulers would not prevent him from building trading posts. In 1524 da Gama was appointed the king's viceroy in India, and he sailed there with another great fleet to take up his post. In December 1524, in Cochin, southwestern India, da Gama fell ill and died.

In 1998, on the five hundredth anniversary of da Gama's first voyage, Indians campaigned against celebrations planned by the Indian and Portuguese governments. Hindus see da Gama as an invader, while Muslims have never forgiven him for the massacre of pilgrims.

SEE ALSO

- Cabral, Pedro Álvares
- Dias, Bartolomeu
- Portugal

GARNIER, FRANCIS

FRANCIS GARNIER WAS BORN on July 25, 1839, in Saint-Etienne, France. A naval officer, colonist, explorer, and cartographer, Garnier is best remembered for his account of his Mekong River expedition (1866–1868), which is an important historical record of the countries his party passed through. He died on December 21, 1873, near the present-day Vietnamese capital of Ho Chi Minh City.

NAVAL AMBITIONS

Francis Garnier enrolled at naval school in 1856. His first posting was in 1860 as an ensign on a trip to China with a French expeditionary force. The following year Garnier traveled to Cochin China, France's colony in the southern part of Vietnam, with Admiral Léonard Charner. After the Battle of Chi Hoa in 1861, Garnier was chosen to take charge of the city of Cho Lon, near Saigon (present-day Ho Chi Minh City).

A TRADE ROUTE TO CHINA

Garnier was eager to aid the expansion of France's empire. He wanted to explore the Mekong River to see if it could serve as a trade route between Cochin China and China. Such a route would greatly increase French influence in the area. Garnier spent much time and energy persuading the French government to support the Mekong expedition.

Eventually, in 1866, his wish was granted. Ernest Doudart de Lagrée, the French representative in Cambodia, was asked to lead the expedition, with Garnier as his deputy. As the expedition's cartographer, Garnier's task was to record the landscape through which the party traveled. Together with Louis Delaporte, a young naval officer, Garnier successfully recorded details of thousands of miles of land around the Mekong River; these notations led to the first maps of this area.

Left **This engraving, based on Francis Garnier's account of the Mekong River expedition, shows a festival taking place in a pagoda (temple) in Laos.**

Above **This map shows the route taken by the Mekong River expedition (1866–1868)**

Exploration of the Mekong River

Lagrée's expedition set out from Saigon in June 1866, finally arriving in China two years later. The journey was tough. The explorers soon realized that the rapids and waterfalls they passed would prevent traders from being able to sail along the Mekong River in even the smallest ship.

Lagrée, Garnier, and their party traveled most of the way in pirogues, narrow canoes that could be dragged overland past rapids. The explorers also had to cope with tiger attacks and dangerous illnesses, such as dysentery and typhoid. Both Lagrée and Garnier became seriously ill with typhoid fever; Garnier survived, but Lagrée was not so fortunate. After Lagrée's death in 1868, Garnier took over the leadership of the expedition. Garnier and his party were unable to reach the source of the Mekong River, but they did become the first Europeans to enter Yunnan Province, in China, from the south.

Destination China

After the Mekong River expedition returned to Saigon, Garnier served in the Franco-German War (1870–1871). Although he fought well, it was suggested that Garnier objected to the peace terms agreed upon after the war and also that he had criticized Lagrée's leadership skills in the Mekong expedition. As a result Garnier failed to win the promotion he felt he deserved. Disappointed, he traveled to China in the hope of improving France's access to trade in tea and silk.

Trouble in Vietnam

Garnier was recalled to Saigon by the French government in 1873. Officially his mission was to find Jean Dupuis, a trader who had opened a new trade route between Vietnam and China and was now attempting to claim land around the Red River. However, some experts believe that Admiral Marie-Jules

July 25, 1839
Francis Garnier is born.

1856
Enrolls at naval school in Brest.

1860
Travels to China as part of a French expeditionary force.

1861
Goes to Saigon and takes part in the Battle of Chi Hoa.

1863
Becomes prefect of Cho Lon.

1866–1868
Explores the Mekong River with Lagrée.

1870–1871
Franco-German War is fought.

1873
Garnier travels up the Red River to Hanoi and joins forces with Jean Dupuis.

December 21, 1873
Is killed when Vietnamese and Chinese forces fight to retake Hanoi.

Dupré, the French governor of Cochin China, supported Dupuis's expansionism. There is evidence that, instead of obeying the wishes of the French government, Admiral Dupré gave Garnier secret orders to work with Dupuis—and not against him.

Together Garnier and Dupuis assembled a small force of French troops and launched an attack on Hanoi, in northern Vietnam. They took control of the city in November 1873, and Garnier's troops also claimed parts of the Red River.

However, the Vietnamese were determined to fight back. A month later, with the help of Chinese bandits, Vietnamese troops stormed Hanoi. During the fighting Francis Garnier was killed. After Garnier's death, Dupré denied that he had encouraged the attack on Hanoi. The French withdrew from northern Vietnam in 1874.

Jean Dupuis *1829–1912*

Dupuis was a French entrepreneur who worked with Francis Garnier to open trade routes in northern Vietnam. After working as a trader in Egypt and China, Dupuis met the members of the Mekong River expedition in 1868. He realized that, since the Mekong River was not navigable, the Red River might serve as a useful trade route in its place. In 1871 Dupuis traveled down the Red River from Yunnan into northern Vietnam. When Dupuis tried to explore the Red River from the south two years later, he met with Vietnamese opposition. Dupuis, Garnier, and a number of troops attacked Hanoi and briefly won control over the area. Soon after, Garnier was killed, and Dupuis returned to France, where he wrote a useful account of the region.

Below **Garnier was killed on December 21, 1873, perhaps by Vietnamese troops .**

SEE ALSO

- France

Geography

SINCE THE EARLIEST TIMES explorers have traveled far from home and brought back new information about what they found. Exploration has thus helped humans reach a better understanding of their world. The study of the physical world and its people and how they interact with one another is called geography.

Early explorers pioneered the study of geography by finding new peoples and places; meanwhile other geographers attempted to make sense of this newly acquired knowledge. By bringing together pieces of the geographical jigsaw, geographers gained a better overall view of the world. Maps were used to record the ever-expanding knowledge base.

Right **In this third-century Roman mosaic the Greek philosopher Anaximander of Miletus (610–c. 547 BCE), often considered the first geographer, is shown with a sundial—one of many ideas he imported from the Middle East.**

495 BCE
The Greek traveler Hecataeus writes *A Tour around the World.*

c. 450 BCE
Herodotus's *History* describes the known world.

c. 245 BCE
Eratosthenes calculates the circumference of the earth.

20 CE
Strabo's *Geography* is published in seventeen volumes.

150
Ptolemy's *Geography* is published.

1154
Al-Idris's *Book of Roger* includes seventy maps produced from accurate coordinates provided by Arab navigators.

1410
Ptolemy's *Geography* is translated into Latin and introduced to Europe.

1418
Henry the Navigator starts a school for navigators in Portugal.

1492
Columbus sails across the Atlantic to the West Indies.

1498
Vasco da Gama pioneers a sea route to India.

The Geography of the Ancient Greeks

The first systematic study of geography began around the sixth century BCE when Greek philosophers began to use a variety of techniques to understand the natural world, including mapping and descriptive writing. Hecataeus, a Greek traveler, used a descriptive approach when he wrote *A Tour around the World* in or about 495 BCE. He had visited Egypt and theorized about the source of the Nile. Although little remains of his writings, they influenced another early Greek geographer, Herodotus (c. 484–424 BCE). Herodotus suggested that several people had traveled far to the south along the coasts of Africa, many centuries before Bartolomeu Dias rounded the Cape of Good Hope in 1488.

The first person to use the word *geography* may have been the Greek mathematician Eratosthenes (c. 276–c. 194 BCE). The word derives from *ge*, meaning "earth," and *graphe*, "description." He was also the first to calculate the circumference of the world—with surprising accuracy. Another Greek who theorized about the shape of the earth was Aristotle (384–322 BCE). From his observations of lunar eclipses (when the earth's shadow is reflected against the moon), he concluded the earth was a sphere.

First Maps of the World

Anaximander of Miletus was the first to attempt to map the world as the Greeks knew it—the Mediterranean was shown surrounded by Europe, part of North Africa, and a small part of western Asia, and all were encircled by a mythical Great Ocean Sea. Eratosthenes' map, drawn in the third century BCE, was the first to include lines of latitude and longitude.

Right **This picture is thought to be of Faxian, a Chinese monk who traveled to India in 399 CE and brought back reports of previously unknown peoples and places.**

1519–1521
Magellan's crew sails around the world.

1569
Mercator's new style of map provides a more accurate view of the globe.

1768–1779
Cook maps the Pacific during his three voyages of discovery.

1830
The Royal Geographical Society is founded in London.

1841–1873
David Livingstone explores Central and Southern Africa.

1860–1861
Burke and Wills cross Australia.

1845–1862
Alexander von Humboldt's *Kosmos* is published

1874
The first university department of geography is established in Germany.

1888
The National Geographic Society is founded in America.

Geography in Roman Times

Herodotus's writings influenced Alexander the Great (356–323 BCE), whose conquests opened up Asia to the Greeks. The Romans learned much about the geography of the Mediterranean from the Greeks and used this knowledge to expand their considerable empire in Europe.

Strabo (c. 64 BCE–20 CE), a Greek historian working for the Roman emperor Augustus, showed how the Romans' view of the world had expanded as a result of their conquests. Strabo's seventeen-volume *Geographia* described the peoples of the known world and thus was one of the first cultural geographies.

Of all the ancient geographers, Ptolemy (c. 100–178 CE), who lived in Alexandria, would have the greatest influence on European navigators and explorers 1,400 years later. In his eight-volume *Geographia,* or *Introduction to the Description of the Earth,* Ptolemy laid down the basic rules of cartography using a grid system of latitude and longitude and calculated the position of over eight thousand places. Ptolemy's biggest mistake was that he underestimated the circumference of the earth by nearly forty percent.

By the second century CE, the Greek and Roman explorers had extended the scope of geographical knowledge from a relatively small area around the eastern Mediterranean to the Atlantic Ocean in the west and China in the east.

Below **This late-sixteenth-century miniature shows astronomers at the Galata observatory, founded in 1557 by Sultan Süleyman I. Under Süleyman, Istanbul, the capital of the Ottoman Empire, became a center of geographical learning.**

China Looks West

On the other side of the world, another great civilization was discovering a world that lay beyond the limits of its knowledge. The Chinese traveler Chang Chien pioneered the Silk Road across central Asia in 138 BCE, and two Buddhist monks, Faxian (c. 399 CE) and Hsuan Tsang (c. 629), traveled to India to study the religious texts there. Other Chinese explorers reached Japan and Taiwan by sea. Chinese mapmakers used a grid system as early as the second century.

The Middle Ages

With the decline of the Roman Empire, travel became more difficult, and for several centuries geographical science did not progress in Europe. Some few Christians insisted that the world should be seen as it was described in the Bible, with Jerusalem positioned at the center of a flat earth. In Europe only the Norse seafarers were making significant geographical discoveries beyond Greenland in 1000 CE.

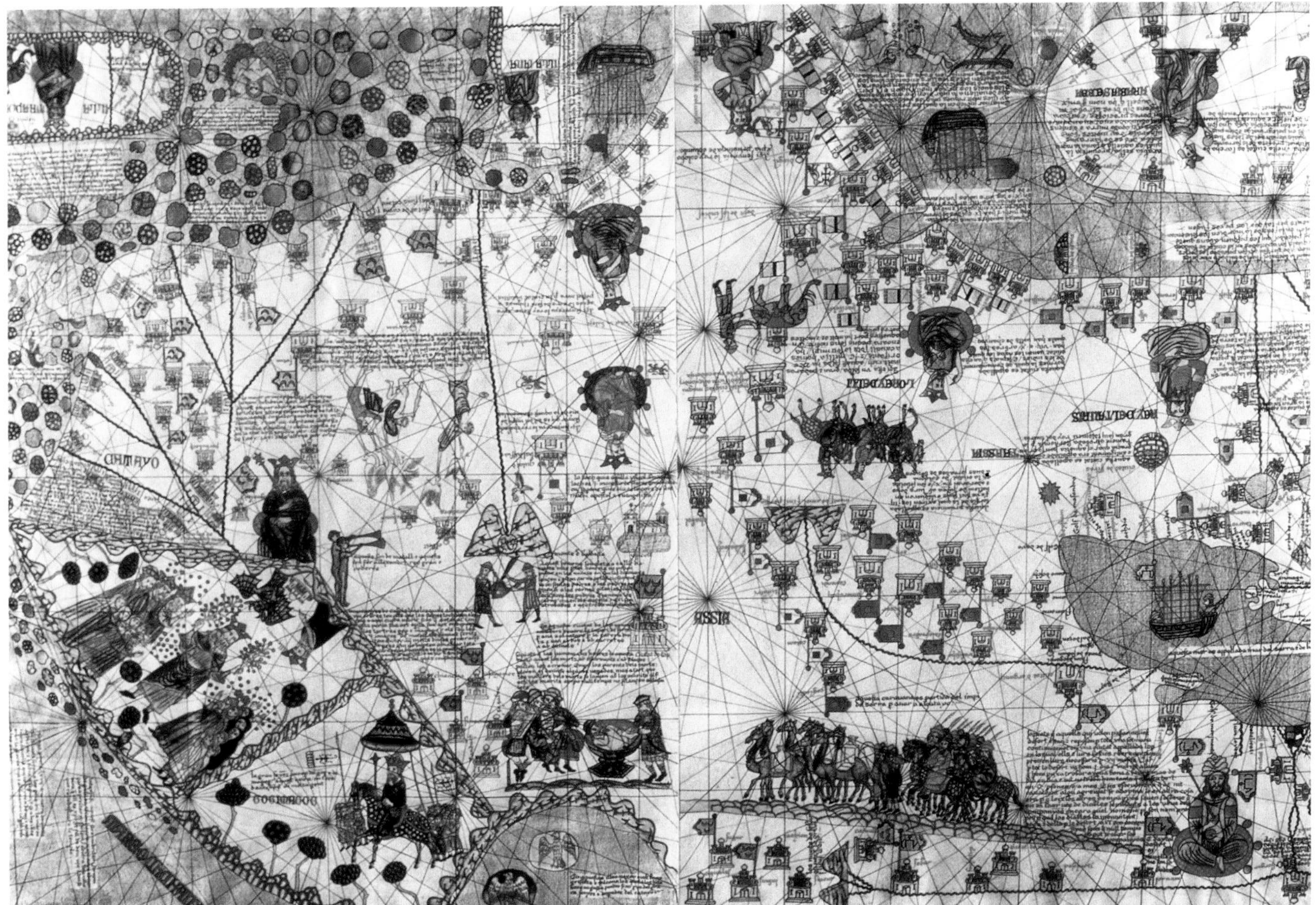

The Viking Leif Eriksson was probably the first European to land in North America around this time.

With the rise of the Arab Muslim empire in the seventh century, the study of geography took a step forward. Arabs had preserved and translated the geographical texts produced by the Greeks and Romans, and by the eighth century they were traveling widely. Arabic geographers improved on the work of the Greeks, especially the maps of Ptolemy.

The most successful explorer of this time was al-Idrisi, who traveled through much of the Islamic world before becoming court geographer to the Christian king Roger II of Sicily. His great work, the *Book of Roger* (1154), gives a fascinating insight into social conditions in Europe and the Middle East during the twelfth century. It also includes some seventy maps based on accurate coordinates supplied by Arab navigators.

By the thirteenth century Venetian traders were beginning to look to the east. Most famous of all Venetian travelers was Marco Polo. The account of his overland journey from Italy to China between 1271 and 1295 revealed to Europeans the extraordinary technical accomplishments of the Chinese as well as their fabulous wealth. Christian missionaries followed, but when central Asia fell into the hands of the Muslims, Europe was denied contact with the east until the fifteenth century.

Above **The Catalan Atlas, produced in 1375, used the most up-to-date sources of geographical information, including Marco Polo's accounts of his travels in Asia.**

Strabo offered a definition of the science of geography, noting that its purpose was

to describe the known parts of the inhabited world . . . to write an assessment of the countries of the world . . . to treat the differences between countries.

Strabo, *Geography,* Vol. II, Books 3–5

Above **Christopher Columbus's 1492 voyage to the Americas with his three ships,the *Pinta, the Niña*, and the *Santa María,* entirely changed the way in which the geography of the world was perceived.**

The Age of Exploration

The fifty years between 1472 and 1522 would witness a revolution in geographical knowledge and people's understanding of the world. At the start of this period, a few Europeans still believed that if a ship sailed too far, it would fall off the edge of the world. By the end, Magellan's crew had made a complete circumnavigation of the globe and thus proved that the world was round.

The roots of this age of discovery lay in the early fifteenth century. In 1410 Ptolemy's flawed *Geographia*—it included several errors, including the suggestion that the Indian Ocean was enclosed by land—was translated into Latin. The magnetic compass was in widespread use, and a grid system of latitude and longitude was being used on maps, although many places were wrongly located. Most educated people believed the world was a sphere, but estimates of its circumference varied considerably.

Prince Henry of Portugal (1394–1460), nicknamed Henry the Navigator, gathered together scholars of all faiths and started collecting maps and manuscripts in what was to become the first geographic research institute in Europe, at Sagres. Navigation techniques were improved and accurate charts compiled from the many voyages Henry sponsored to explore the west coast of Africa between 1436 and 1460.

The achievements of these coastal navigators were followed by the pioneering voyage of Vasco da Gama to India around the Cape of Good Hope. Throughout the sixteenth century Portuguese fleets sailed farther and farther east. By 1511 the Portuguese had a trading base at Malacca on the Malaysian peninsula, and in 1542 they reached Japan.

Christopher Columbus wanted to reach Asia by sailing west. He had read the writings of Ptolemy and Marco Polo, as well as other geographical works, and came to the conclusion that the circumference of the earth was much smaller than had previously been thought. He argued hard with both Portuguese and Spanish geographers, who were convinced he would fail, before persuading the Spanish monarchs Ferdinand V and Isabella I to sponsor his 1492 voyage.

By the time Columbus died, most geographers realized the world was actually much larger than they had thought and that a new continent lay between Europe and Asia. Within the next twenty years much of the east coast of North and South America was mapped. Between 1521 and the death of Cook in 1779 the outline of the world was gradually drawn.

New Maps for a New World

New kinds of maps were needed to depict the new discoveries. The first globe, produced by Martin Behaim in 1492, showed the east coast of Asia in place of the east coast of North America. The first printed map to show the Americas was drawn by Martin Waldseemüller in 1507. The challenge of navigating long distances was solved in 1569, when Gerardus Mercator developed a map projection that sailors could easily use with a compass. By 1630 this projection was used by most navigators in low and middle latitudes, and a more accurate way of recording new discoveries was achieved.

New Frontiers

Since the time of the ancient Greeks, there had been rumors of a great southern continent. The Dutch discovery of Australia in 1606 was quickly followed by Abel Tasman's voyages to Tasmania and New Zealand. James Cook's three voyages, which led to the mapping of the Pacific, eventually proved that a great southern continent did not exist.

Left **The first mapmaker to show the round earth as a globe was Martin Behaim of Nuremberg in 1492, but he significantly underestimated the size of the earth's circumference.**

By 1800 the coastlines of all the major continents, except Antarctica, had been mapped by explorers and navigators. The new challenge for geographers was to fill in the blanks in the interior of the continents, particularly Africa. Rivers were thought to provide navigable waterways, and explorers attempted to follow the courses of the Niger, Nile, and Congo, suffering great hardships in the process. In North America the Missouri and Colorado Rivers and their tributaries were mapped.

Below **Varenius, the author of the first geography textbook, may have been the model for Vermeer's *The Geographer* (1668–1669).**

By the beginning of the twentieth century, attention turned again to the Polar regions, and the exploration of Antarctica began. Soon airplanes not only revolutionized access to remote regions but also enabled new aerial mapping techniques.

Modern Geography

Explorers have contributed greatly to understanding of the world, and all could be called geographers. However, the existence of geography as a separate academic discipline is relatively recent. Two German geographers, Alexander von Humboldt and Carl Ritter, who both lived in Berlin in the mid-nineteenth century, are considered to be the founders of modern geography. Both produced works that brought together the achievements of the explorers and used new ideas and methods of study to put them into context.

Carl Ritter, a brilliant and influential lecturer, worked largely from other people's observations. Humboldt was an outstanding scientist-explorer who produced a thirty-volume work as a result of his expeditions in South America. He also wrote *Kosmos*, in which he brought together his innovative ideas about the interconnectedness of people, places, and events.

Before the 1830s geography had been a subject that one person could try to master in a lifetime. Around this time geography was first taught in universities as a subject in its own right. The body of geographical knowledge grew so large that fields of specialization began to appear. Individual geographers came together to form clubs and societies to share their knowledge and initiate larger projects.

The Royal Geographical Society (RGS) was founded in 1830, followed fifty years later by America's National Geographic Society. Both have had a profound influence on geography and exploration. The RGS sponsored many expeditions to resolve some of the big questions challenging geographers, such as the location of the source of the Nile and the existence of the Northwest Passage. Both societies continue to sponsor geographical research expeditions.

Modern geographers view the world from many different vantage points. Some geographers are still explorers working in remote and challenging environments and trying to improve understanding of the world. New technologies allow access to areas previously unable to support human life—the deep ocean and space. For those with an enquiring mind, there remains plenty to explore closer to home, and the challenge for geographers—to understand the interrelationship of people with their environments in a changing world—is as great as ever.

The First Geography Textbook

The first general textbook on geography is usually credited to Bernhardus Varenius. His *Geographia Generalis*, written in 1650, became the standard work for the next hundred years. To Varenius the discipline of geography was both theoretical and practical, and he divided the subject into three distinct branches. The first concerned the dimensions of the earth; the second (physical geography) covered the effects of climate and tides; and the third (cultural geography) dealt with peoples of the world.

SEE ALSO

• Alexander the Great • Columbus, Christopher • Cook, James
• Dias, Bartolomeu • Eratosthenes of Cyrene • Faxian • Gama, Vasco da
• Henry the Navigator • Humboldt, Alexander von • Latitude and Longitude
• Leif Eriksson • Magellan, Ferdinand • Mapmaking • Map Projection
• Mercator, Gerardus • Ptolemy • Silk Road • Southern Continent • Strabo

Glenn, John

JOHN HERSCHEL GLENN, born on July 18, 1921, in Cambridge, Ohio, took part in two historic events in the history of space travel. In 1962 Glenn became the first American astronaut to orbit the earth, and in 1998 he became the oldest explorer to travel in space.

Below **For his mission to orbit the earth, named Mercury-Atlas 6 (MA-6), Glenn wore an innovative space suit designed to protect him in the event of a failure in the cabin pressure.**

Military Background

John Glenn grew up in New Concord, Ohio, where he also attended school and college. In 1942 he enrolled in the Naval Aviation Cadet Program, and the following year he was commissioned by the U.S. Marine Corps. A skilled pilot, Glenn flew over 150 missions during World War II and the Korean War and won several medals for bravery. He subsequently worked as a test pilot, for which job he was required to fly new and experimental aircraft. In 1959 Glenn was selected to train as an astronaut by the directors of NASA's Project Mercury.

It was as part of Project Mercury that NASA launched the first manned U.S. space flights, which took place between 1961 and 1963. On May 5, 1961, Alan B. Shepard became the first American to fly into space; he was followed on July 21, 1961, by Virgil I. Grissom. However, neither Shepard nor Grissom had traveled around the earth, as the Soviet cosmonaut Yury Gagarin had done in April 1961. Having acted as a back-up astronaut for the first two Project Mercury flights, in 1962 John Glenn was finally given his chance to explore space on a mission whose objective was to orbit the earth.

July 18, 1921
John Glenn is born.

1943
Joins the U.S. Marine Corps.

1954
Becomes a test pilot.

1959
Trains as an astronaut.

February 20, 1962
Becomes the first U.S. astronaut to orbit the earth.

1964
Retires from the space program.

1974
Is elected a senator from Ohio.

October 29–November 7, 1998
At the age of 77, becomes the oldest person to travel in space.

March 1, 1999
The NASA Lewis Research Center is renamed the NASA John H. Glenn Research Center.

Blast Off

On February 20, 1962, Glenn was launched from Cape Canaveral in Florida. He traveled into space in a capsule named *Friendship 7*, which was attached to a powerful Atlas rocket. Glenn orbited the earth not once but three times. He reached a maximum altitude of 162 miles (261 km) and a speed of approximately 17,500 miles per hour (28,163 kph), and for all but seven minutes of his journey, he was weightless. When he splashed down near the Bahamas 4 hours, 55 minutes, and 23 seconds after takeoff, he was given a hero's welcome.

"A Real Fireball!"

John Glenn's historic space journey in 1962 did not go quite as planned. After his first orbit an engineer on earth realized that the space capsule's heat shield was not fixed firmly in position. If the heat shield became detached, *Friendship 7* would have little protection from the blistering temperatures objects experience when entering the earth's atmosphere, and the space capsule would be destroyed. While Glenn continued his journey, those in the control center on earth worked out the best plan of action. They decided to proceed with the landing but did not tell Glenn to jettison any equipment, for fear of losing the heat shield at the same time. Although the outer coating of *Friendship 7* caught fire, Glenn survived reentry. After his capsule was safely plucked out of the Atlantic Ocean, Glenn described the journey back to earth as "a real fireball of a ride!"

Below **Glenn boards *Friendship 7* for his historic 1962 space flight.**

Above **This photo was taken before Glenn's second space flight, on board the space shuttle *Discovery*, in 1998.**

THE OLDEST PERSON IN SPACE

Glenn retired from NASA in 1964 to follow a career in business and later politics. First elected senator from Ohio in 1974, he was re-elected three times.

At the age of 77, Glenn was given the chance to travel to space once more, this time on board the space shuttle *Discovery*. His mission was to take part in research on aging, sponsored by NASA and the National Institute on Aging.

When astronauts adapt to the weightlessness in space, they often experience health problems that are similar to those suffered by people as they grow older. Symptoms include the loss of bone and muscle, balance problems, and sleep disorders. During mission STS-95, Glenn took part in experiments to help scientists explore the aging process in the hope that, in the future, new technologies might be developed to help people stay healthier as they age. Glenn spent almost nine days in space, orbited the earth 134 times, and traveled 3.6 million miles (5.8 million km). In 1999, in honor of Glenn's contribution to space exploration, the NASA Lewis Research Center was renamed the NASA John H. Glenn Research Center.

On January 16, 1998, came the announcement of the decision to send John Glenn to space for a second time on board the space shuttle *Discovery*.

What an incredible day for John Glenn, for Ohio, for NASA, but most of all, for America, because the man who almost thirty-six years ago climbed into the Friendship 7 and showed the boundless promise for a new generation, is now poised to show the world that senior citizens have the right stuff.

Dan Goldin, NASA administrator, 1992–2001

SEE ALSO

- Gagarin, Yury
- NASA
- Shepard, Alan B., Jr.
- Spacecraft
- Space Exploration

Global Positioning System

THE GLOBAL POSITIONING SYSTEM (GPS) is a navigation system, controlled by orbiting satellites, that enables a person to know his or her exact location anywhere on or above the earth's surface. Originally developed for the U.S. military, GPS can now be used by anyone who has the appropriate equipment.

Finding the Way

Throughout history explorers have found their way around the world using different navigational aids. Observations with the naked eye, the magnetic compass, the sextant, and the chronometer were all used by navigators and explorers at various times throughout history to calculate their position or the direction in which they were heading. Some methods were more accurate than others, but until the twentieth century, none was capable of pinpointing a position with absolute precision.

Radio-based Navigation

Radio-based navigation systems, first developed in the early twentieth century, work by sending radio waves on certain frequencies in certain directions. When a wave is picked up by a ship, crew members measure its frequency, from which they can calculate their distance and direction relative to the origin of the signal and so plot their position. However, there are drawbacks. High-frequency radio waves travel in a straight line, and because the surface of the earth is curved, they transmit well only over short distances. When the transmitter and the receiver become too far apart, the horizon will eventually interrupt the signal. Low-frequency radio waves can be transmitted over longer distances, because they travel in a curved line. However, because they bounce around a lot, the signal is distorted and loses its accuracy.

Eventually it was realized that a radio system positioned in space would provide reliable data for the entire planet; transmitters and receivers would not be interrupted by obstacles on the surface of the earth and by the curvature of the earth itself, as high-frequency radio waves sent from space would fan out to cover a large circular area. The new space-based system was given the name Global Positioning System (GPS).

Launch

Navstar 1, the first GPS satellite, was launched in February 1978 and put into orbit about 12,500 miles (20,000 km) above the earth. However, it was another seventeen years before the U.S. Defense Department announced that the multibillion dollar system was fully operational. GPS was designed for the U.S. military; although civilian use was permitted, errors deliberately programmed into the system reduced the accuracy of nonmilitary readings. It was not until May 2000 that this practice was abandoned.

GLONASS

GPS is not the only space-based navigational system in the world. The Russian equivalent of GPS is called GLONASS (Global Orbiting Navigation Satellite System). Operated by the Ministry of Defense of the Russian Federation, it uses twenty-four satellites of its own, which orbit earth about 620 miles (1,000 km) lower than GPS satellites.

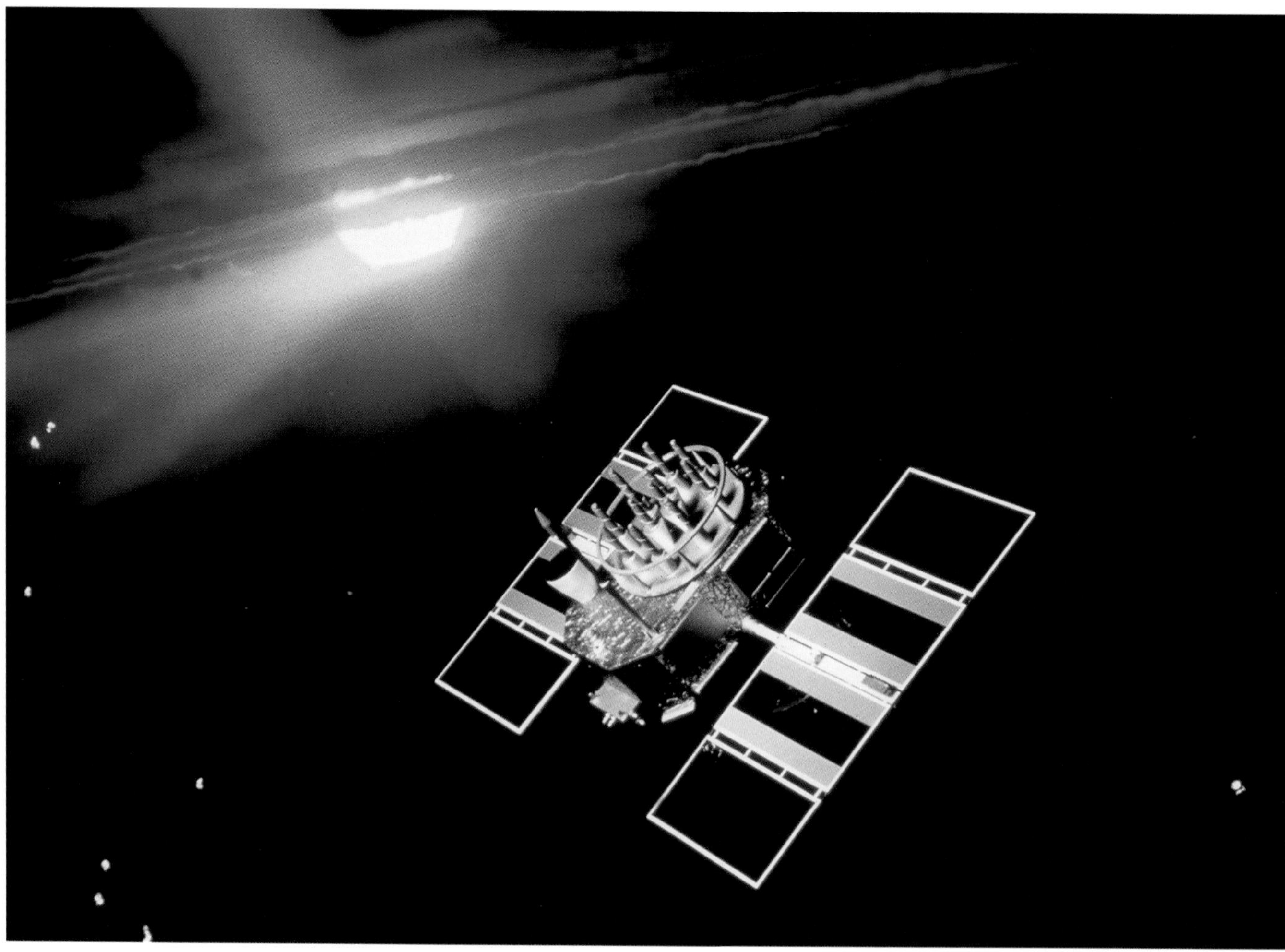

Above **An artist's impression of *GPS-12*, one of the global positioning satellites that orbits the earth.**

How GPS Works

Twenty-four GPS satellites orbit the earth. Signals from these satellites can be picked up by portable receivers carried by ships, airplanes, cars, and people anywhere on earth. Travelers can use these signals to identify their precise location.

The radio wave signals sent by each GPS satellite travel at the speed of light and include details of the exact time the signal was sent. When a portable receiver on earth receives a signal from a GPS satellite, it measures the difference between the time encoded in the signal and the time that this signal reaches the portable receiver. The receiver can then calculate the distance between itself and the satellite.

Because there are so many GPS satellites orbiting the earth, wherever a receiver is positioned, it will have access to data from at least four satellite signals. The signals from three satellites are needed to work out latitude, longitude, and—crucial for explorers in mountainous regions and for pilots—elevation. A fourth satellite improves the accuracy of the reading from the other three.

Control stations on earth make sure that the GPS satellites orbiting the planet are working properly. They also make sure that the clock contained in each satellite is adjusted to exactly the right time to ensure the accuracy of the data transmitted.

1920s
Radio-based navigation systems are developed.

1957
The USSR launches the first man-made satellite, called *Sputnik*.

1978
The first GPS satellite is launched.

1994
The twenty-fourth GPS satellite is launched.

1995
The U.S. Defense Department announces that the GPS system is complete and fully operational.

Right **This field geologist is using a handheld GPS receiver to check his location.**

Anywhere on Earth

As the twenty-first century began, many civil engineers were using GPS instead of traditional surveying equipment to plan the positioning of new roads and structures. The crew of a ship or an airplane can use GPS to work out its position even when the sky is cloudy. GPS receivers are also built into many modern automobiles. The receivers are often linked to electronic maps, which use GPS data to indicate to drivers where they are and direct them to where they want to go.

Hikers and walkers also benefit from GPS—they can check their exact position any time and anywhere. They do not even have to carry cumbersome receiver equipment; wristwatches containing GPS receivers were available for the first time at the end of the twentieth century.

Early devices and methods for calculating a person's position, although ingenious, were extremely complex and often clumsy to use. Modern-day explorers, on the other hand, can work out their exact position at the touch of a button. This fact was dramatically demonstrated in 1985, when the oceanographer Dr. Robert Ballard found the remains of the RMS *Titanic*, which was presumed lost forever. He recorded the location of the *Titanic* using the GPS system and was able to return directly to the wreck on his next visit.

Satellite Positions

GPS satellites orbit the earth at a height of about 12,660 miles (20,370 km) in an asynchronous orbit. That is, they pass overhead at different times of the day. Geostationary satellites—for example, communications satellites—travel in a much higher orbit so that they are always positioned over the same point on the earth's surface, and thus each can serve a particular area of the earth. As each GPS satellite does exactly the same job as every other GPS satellite, it is not necessary for them to remain above the same part of the earth; a GPS receiver on earth will receive its bearings from whichever three or four satellites it can most readily access.

SEE ALSO

- Chronometer
- Dead Reckoning
- Navigation
- Navigational Instruments
- Satellites

GREAT BRITAIN

AS NO POINT IN the British Isles is far from the sea, the peoples of these islands have long traditions of maritime exploration. Early sea captains sailed in search of plunder but also found new lands and advanced understanding of the world. Later explorers ranged across the British Empire, some driven by curiosity and others by the search for new resources. In the twentieth century prominent Britons were among the first people to reach the world's most inaccessible places.

In the Service of the Crown

Early British monarchs understood the importance of sea power. The Scots king James IV (reigned 1488–1513) built a powerful fleet to advance trade and explore the northern seas. Elizabeth I of England (reigned 1558–1603) encouraged her most daring sea captains, such as John Hawkins and Francis Drake, to trade overseas and also to plunder enemy ships when they had the chance.

Right **This map of the coast of Virginia shows dangers both real (treacherous reefs) and imaginary (sea monsters).**

1500–1605
English ships are active in Arctic and American waters.

1600–1700
British colonize the Americas.

1785–1820
British explorers chart northwestern Canada.

1750–1850
British map the Pacific, Australia, and New Zealand and search for a northwest passage. African Association sponsors expeditions to follow the Niger River.

1850–1910
British missionaries are active in Africa. Explorers search for sources of the Nile River.

1875–1953
British explorers travel in the Middle East and central Asia. British scientists explore the Antarctic. First ascent of Mount Everest by British-led team.

Above **During the nineteenth century, many British explorers searched for a northwest passage. In 1818, the Admiralty instructed David Buchan and John Franklin to sail as close to the North Pole as possible in an attempt to find a direct sea route to Asia through the Arctic Ocean.**

As well as capturing Spanish treasure, British navigators gathered important geographical information about the New World. The privateer William Dampier (1651–1715) was also a skilled hydrographer who charted the currents and trade winds of the Pacific on his three voyages around the world. Others, such as Sir Walter Raleigh (1554–1618), hoped to build new colonies overseas. On several voyages between 1601 and 1611, Christopher Newport carried settlers to Jamestown, Virginia, which became the first English colony in North America. Farther north, Sir William Alexander established New Scotland (Nova Scotia) in 1621.

Searching for the Northwest Passage

In the sixteenth century English explorers tried to find an Arctic sea route to the Pacific, hoping to use this northwest passage to bring valuable goods from the east directly to the markets of Europe. Martin Frobisher and Henry Hudson each made three voyages into the frozen north, but Frobisher found only some low-value ores, while Hudson died after a mutiny, cast adrift in an open boat.

In 1845 Sir John Franklin renewed the search for a northwest passage. Franklin's expedition vanished, though Inuit hunters found several dead Europeans in the ice. The sea route was finally discovered by John Rae, who came from the Orkney Islands. Rae worked with the local Inuit in order to learn how to survive in the Canadian Arctic wild. A cairn at Rae Strait, north of Boothia Peninsula, commemorates his discovery in 1854 of the last part of the Northwest Passage.

Exploring an Empire

In the eighteenth century Britain and France fought for control of the world's trade routes. Victory in the Seven Years' War (1756–1763) ensured British control of North America, India, and the Pacific and marked the beginning of a great surge in British exploration.

The British in Canada

In Canada in 1789, the Scottish explorer Alexander Mackenzie discovered the river that carries his name and became the first European to cross the Rockies. Simon Fraser, following in Mackenzie's footsteps, opened up a vast tract of western Canada, which he named New Caledonia after the Latin name for Scotland. Many of the trading posts in northern Canada were founded by the British fur trader David Thompson between 1797 and 1812, while the western Canadian seaboard was accurately mapped by George Vancouver in the 1790s.

The eastern coast of Australia was surveyed by James Cook in 1770, and the continent was circumnavigated by Matthew Flinders between 1801 and 1803. The first land crossing from south to north was made by an Irishman, Robert Burke, and an Englishman, William Wills, in 1860 and 1861. Both men died on the return journey.

In 1853 and 1854 the English scholar Sir Richard Burton disguised himself as a Muslim and entered the holy city of Mecca. In 1857, searching for the source of the Nile with John Hanning Speke, he found Lake Tanganyika (in present-day Tanzania). Some explorers were also botanists: plants gathered by Joseph Banks in Canada and the Pacific formed the basis of the Natural History Museum in London, while Allan Cunningham's Australian plant collections were included in the Royal Botanic Gardens at Kew.

In Search of Souls

In the nineteenth century a new kind of explorer left Britain's shores for distant lands. These explorers were Christian missionaries sponsored by agencies, such as the London Missionary Society, that sought to carry the Christian message "among heathen and other unenlightened nations" in Africa.

David Livingstone, from Blantyre near Glasgow, made several epic journeys through southern and Central Africa to establish Christian missions and attempt to bring about the end of the slave trade. Mary Slessor from Dundee traveled widely through West Africa's Calabar coast and cared for the local people there. Known as "the great mother," she was much loved. Another woman, Annie Royle Taylor, traveled a thousand miles (1,600 km) across Tibet in an attempt to bring Christianity to the city of Lhasa.

Below **This 1771 painting commemorates the successful expedition to Australia by James Cook (center) and Joseph Banks. Beside them stands Lord Sandwich, the first lord of the Admiralty, who supported their expedition to the Pacific.**

In Africa, the anthropologist Mary Henrietta Kingsley (1862–1900) made one of the century's most dangerous voyages. Canoeing up the Ogooué River, she met the Fang, a tribe feared for its practice of cannibalism.

To the Ends of the Earth

By 1900 most of the world, except for the Poles and the more extreme mountain ranges, had been mapped. Many Britons dreamed of planting the Union Jack at the South Pole. On January 17, 1912, Robert Falcon Scott, a naval officer, and his weary comrades, dragging their sleds, reached the Pole only to find that the Norwegian Roald Amundsen had been there a month earlier. The bravery, self-sacrifice, and ultimate death of Scott and his men is one of the most moving stories of polar exploration.

Ernest Shackleton also made several Antarctic voyages. When his ship *Endurance* was crushed by pack ice and sunk in 1915, Shackleton led his men to Elephant Island and then sailed eight hundred miles (1,280 km) to South Georgia in search of help.

British traditions of exploring have been maintained by Ranulph Fiennes, who has led over thirty expeditions to the Poles, including the first polar circumnavigation of the globe, which was completed in 1982.

SEE ALSO

• Banks, Joseph • Bishop, Isabella Lucy
• Burke, Robert O'Hara • Burton, Richard Francis
• Cook, James • Dampier, William • Drake, Francis
• Flinders, Matthew • Franklin, John
• Frobisher, Martin • Hillary, Edmund
• Hudson, Henry • Livingstone, David
• Mackenzie, Alexander • Northwest Passage
• Park, Mungo • Raleigh, Walter
• Scott, Robert Falcon • Shackleton, Ernest Henry
• Speke, John Hanning • Thompson, David
• Vancouver, George

Mount Everest

British adventurers have a strong association with the world's highest mountain. George Mallory and Andrew Irvine disappeared in 1924 near the top of Mount Everest. The British Everest Expedition under Colonel John Hunt claimed the first successful ascent of the mountain when Edmund Hillary and Tenzing Norgay stepped onto Everest's summit on May 29, 1953.

Below **Fearless explorer Mary Kingsley traveled up the Ogooué River (in present-day Gabon) and collected fish for the British Museum.**

Gudrid

GUDRIDUR THORBJARNARSDOTTIR, a Norse woman who lived around 1000 CE, was a Christian at a time when Christianity had only recently been introduced to Iceland. According to sagas (epic tales from Norse literature) that give details of her life, she sailed from Greenland to North America on a colonizing expedition with her husband. There she gave birth to a son, Snorri Thorfinnsson, who became the first child of European descent born on the American continent.

Right **This statue of Gudrid and her son Snorri was unveiled by the president of Iceland in 2000.**

c. 985
Gudrid is born in Iceland.

c. 1000
Settles in Greenland with her father.

c. 1007–8
After the death of her husband, Thorstein Eriksson, Gudrid marries Thorfinn Karlsefni.

c. 1009
Sails with Karlsefni from Iceland to North America; in the autumn of 1009 or 1010, gives birth to Snorri.

c. 1013
Returns to Greenland with her family.

AFTER 1015
Moves to Iceland; visits Norway; visits Rome, Italy; returns to Iceland and becomes a nun.

Gudrid and the Fortune-Teller

Gudrid Thorbjarnarsdottir (her surname means "Thorbjarn's daughter") was the daughter of Hallveig Einarsdottir and Thorbjarn Vifilsson, an important farmer in Iceland. Gudrid's upbringing was left to a family friend, Orm, who brought her up as his foster child. While Gudrid was a teenager, there came a time of hardship, and when Thorbjarn's farm suffered, he moved to Greenland, where his friend Erik the Red had built a settlement. With him went Gudrid, described as "a most beautiful woman—accomplished at everything she did or was." On Greenland, Gudrid was asked to help a pagan (non-Christian) woman foretell the future. Although Gudrid refused, declaring she was a Christian, she was put under pressure to chant a spell. The fortune-teller predicted that Gudrid would marry on Greenland and that although her marriage would not last, she would eventually see happiness and a "goodly progeny" in Iceland.

Gudrid's Two Husbands

According to the account given in the sagas, Gudrid married Thorstein Eriksson in 1006. He was a son of Erik the Red and the brother of Freydis Eriksdottir and Leif and Thorvald Eriksson. The couple was married at Brattahlid, Greenland. However, just as the fortune-teller had predicted, the marriage came to a tragic end; in the winter of 1007/1008, Thorstein died during an outbreak of the plague. Afterward Gudrid was taken in by Thorstein's brother Leif, who cared for her. In the autumn of 1008, a wealthy trader from Iceland, Thorfinn Thordarsson, whose nickname was Karlsefni, came to Greenland and married Gudrid soon after Christmas.

Gudrid Travels to Vinland

In the spring of about 1009, Karlsefni sailed with at least three ships from Greenland to Vinland (the coast of present-day Newfoundland), a land first explored by Leif and Thorvald Eriksson, where Karlsefni planned to establish a permanent colony. Gudrid sailed with Karlsefni, together with up to 160 people and their livestock. After two days they reached a land of flat stones. According to the *Saga of Erik the Red*, they named this land Helluland, meaning "flatstone land" (present-day Baffin Island). From there they sailed to a forested shoreline that they

A Norse Settlement in North America

In the 1960s the archaeologists Helge and Ann Stine Ingstad discovered a Norse settlement on the northern tip of Newfoundland, at L'Anse aux Meadows. It was a major discovery, for it proved that America had been reached by Norse travelers, just as the sagas claimed. Until then historians had doubted whether the sagas were reliable historical records. The uncovering of eight buildings and artifacts in North America, identical to ones from Greenland, Iceland, and Scandinavia, was certain evidence of Norse contact. The L'Anse aux Meadows settlement, dated to between 1000 and 1100, could have supported up to ninety people. It may be the one the sagas say was built by Thorfinn Karlsefni, where Gudrid gave birth to Snorri Thorfinnsson. Equally, it may have begun as the settlement of Leif Eriksson and been later expanded by Karlsefni. Alternatively, it could be a settlement not recorded in the sagas at all.

Below **Reconstructed Norse buildings at L'Anse aux Meadows, Newfoundland.**

named Markland (present-day Labrador) and then on to Vinland. It is not clear if these places are the same as or different from the ones given identical names by Leif Eriksson some ten years previously. It is believed that Karlsefni's expedition reached present-day Newfoundland, where a settlement was established. The sagas say Karlsefni called the settlement Hop, meaning "tidal pool." Its location is unknown.

The House That Snorri Built?

In an excavation on Iceland in 2002, U.S. archaeologists discovered the remains of a thousand-year-old longhouse (farmhouse) from the Norse period of the island's history. Measuring 95 feet (29 m) in length and 30 feet (9 m) in width, with turf walls 5 feet (1.5 m) thick, it was occupied between 1000 and 1100. It is located on Iceland's north coast in an area where Snorri Thorfinnsson is believed to have lived, and the excavators have speculated that it is his farmhouse.

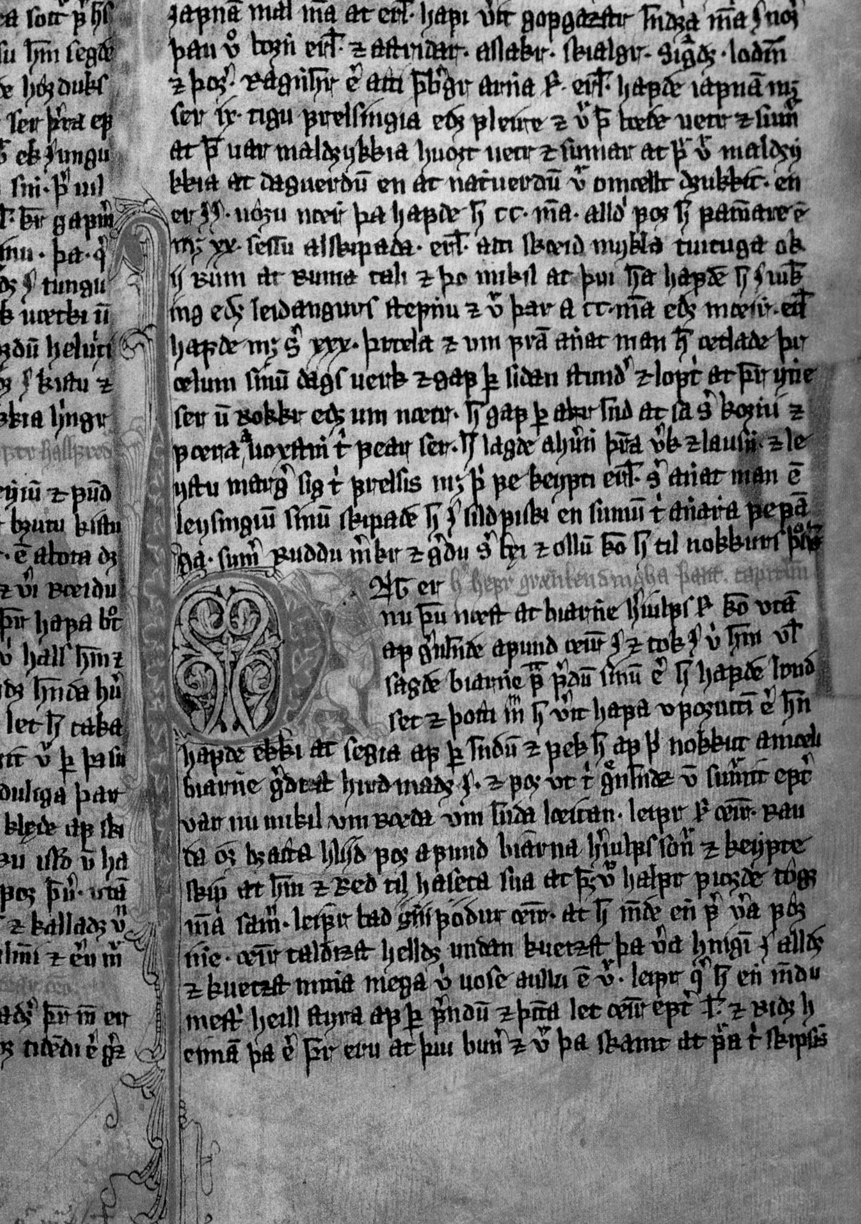

Left **A page from a Norse saga, written in Iceland in the 1300s. Documents such as this one reveal valuable information about Norse explorers that, in some cases, can be matched with archaeological evidence.**

Birth of Gudrid's Son

Gudrid gave birth to a son in the first autumn of her arrival in Vinland, around 1009 or 1010. Named Snorri Thorfinnsson, he was the first child of European parents born in North America. The family remained in Vinland for three years, but as relations with the Native Americans (called Skraelings by the Norse) became hostile, Karlsefni abandoned the settlement and led his people back to Greenland with a valuable cargo of goods (animal skins, timber, and berries).

After two years on Greenland, Gudrid, Karlsefni, and Snorri moved to Iceland, and while there, Gudrid and her husband apparently visited Norway. Together they had at least one more son, Bjorn (or Thorbjorn). As the fortune-teller foretold, their children had many famous descendants. After the death of Karlsefni, Gudrid is said to have made a pilgrimage to Rome, Italy. Late in life she became a nun and recluse.

SEE ALSO

- Erik the Red • Leif Eriksson • Scandinavia
- Vikings

GLOSSARY

botulism A serious form of food poisoning caused by eating preserved food that has been contaminated with botulinum organisms.

cartography The science and art of mapmaking.

Crusade One of several Christian military expeditions, especially in the eleventh, twelfth, and thirteenth centuries, whose purpose was to regain the Holy Land from the Muslims.

dysentery An infection that causes severe diarrhea.

entrepreneur A person who, often at some risk, sets up a business.

expeditionary force A group of explorers, usually army or navy officers.

geology The study of the origin and structure of the earth.

grid A network of parallel lines intersecting at right angles to produce a series of identical squares.

hydrography Study of seas, lakes, and rivers, especially the charting of tides or the measurement of river flow.

midshipman Temporary rank held by young men training to be naval officers.

Moor Member of a Muslim people of mixed North African, Berber, and Spanish descent who ruled Spain from the tenth to the thirteenth centuries.

Norse Referring generally to the people of Scandinavia (Norway, Sweden, and Denmark), especially during the years 790 to 1100.

oceanography Scientific study of the oceans.

orbit An object's regularly repeated path around a star or planet.

peninsula A long, narrow piece of land that juts into the sea or a lake.

philology The scientific study of the history of languages and their relationship to one another, especially based on an analysis of texts.

pilgrim One who travels to visit a holy place.

pinnace A light sailing ship, often used to carry provisions or messages from one ship to another or from ship to shore.

privateer A privately-owned ship hired by a government to attack and raid the ships of another country; also, a crew member of such a ship.

projection A method of displaying the curvature of the earth on a flat surface so that its physical features can be seen in true relation to each other.

Reconquista The centuries-long Spanish campaign to drive out the Moors, the descendants of the Muslims who had conquered Spain in the eighth century.

saga A heroic Icelandic family history meant to demonstrate the correct and honorable way to behave. Sagas began as word-of-mouth stories and were written between 1100 and 1500 in Iceland or sometimes in Norway.

Sanskrit An ancient language of the Indian subcontinent, considered the root of many modern European and Asian languages.

satellite An object, natural or artificial, that orbits a planet.

Skraeling A Norse word, meaning "wretch" or "ugly person," used to describe the native North Americans the Icelandic settlers encountered.

solstice The time during summer and winter when the sun is vertically above the point that represents its farthest distance north or south of the equator. In the Northern Hemisphere the summer solstice is reached around June 21, and the winter solstice around December 22.

stade An ancient unit of length used by Greek and Roman surveyors; the standard length of a stade is generally assumed to be six hundred feet (965 m), though many variations exist.

topography The physical features of an area, such as mountains, valleys, and streams; also, the study and mapping of such features.

typhoid A severe infection that causes a rash and stomach pains.

Viking A term, from a Norwegian word meaning both "pirate" and "warfare," used generally to refer to a Scandinavian (someone from Norway, Sweden, or Denmark) during the years 790 to 1100; especially, any of the Norse raiders who plundered the coasts of western Europe in that period.

INDEX

Page numbers in **boldface** type refer to main articles. Page numbers in *italic* type refer to illustrations.